My Vision from God

Charmyne Fluker

MY VISION FROM GOD
Copyright © 2021 by Charmyne Fluker

All rights reserved. No part of this publication may be reproduced, distributed, or transmitted in any form or by any means, including photocopying, recording, or other electronic or mechanical methods, without the prior written permission of the publisher or author, except in the case of brief quotations embodied in critical reviews and certain other noncommercial uses permitted by copyright law.

Although every precaution has been taken to verify the accuracy of the information contained herein, the author and publisher assume no responsibility for any errors or omissions. No liability is assumed for damages that may result from the use of information contained within.

Library of Congress Control Number: 2021914879
ISBN-13:   Paperback: 978-1-64749-567-1
          ePub: 978-1-64749-568-8

Printed in the United States of America

GoToPublish LLC
1-888-337-1724
www.gotopublish.com
info@gotopublish.com

Dedication Letter

First I would like to give Honor and Praise to the Lord Jesus Christ who is the Lord of my Life. I want to dedicate this book to my sons Kevin and Jerry Fluker, also a special person in my life, my Mother Lillian Essex Moran. Who has been a blessing to me. In addition, I would like to thank God for all my Brothers and Sisters, and all who were raised in my Mother's home.

Contents

Dedication Letter iii
Acknowledgments ix
Introduction 1
All Those People 7
Caught Up 8
Caught Up 11
Get Up and Go Home 12
Husband And Wife 15
God Bless America 16
God Chose the Season 18
God Chose The Season 21
I Never Done Nothing Wrong 22
None Is Righteous 22
I Never Done Nothing Wrong 26
Perfect Peace 28
Perfect Peace 32
Jesus Calms A Storm 33
The Beauty of Praise and Worship 34
The Beauty of Praise and Worship 37
The Table Is Set 38
The Table Is Set 40
Unconditional Love 41
The Gift of Love 47
Unconditional Love 49
When Your Back Is Against 50
When Your Back Is Against The Wall 53

Part II
Stories without Poems

Are You A Slave? 55
Benefits 58
March 8, 1999 60
Go Pass to Excel 61
He Spared Us 63
I Messed Around and Fell in Love 64
It's Just a Loan 66
Open House 68
Ready or Not Here I Come 71
Real Vs Reality 75
Someone Called Me 79
S-S-S-S 80
The Instructions 83
The Satan Presentation 85
Walking With Christ 91
When Jesus Returns What Will You Be Doing? 94
Would You Do It? 98
The Will 101

Part III
Poems

Amazing Grace 105
Drip!!!! 106
Every Man for Himself 107
Going Away 108
He Is... 109
He's All That 110
I- Me- My 111
It's Me O' Lord Standing In The Need Of Prayer Again! 112
Last Moment Notice 113
Love 114
Thanks 115
Want To Be 116
You're Not 117

Just A Little Something Extra

Seasons of Love 120

Our First 121
The Day 122
Just A Thought
Children Learn What They Live 124
The Lord's Prayer 126
References 127
About the Author 128

Acknowledgments

This that I write unto you hopefully this book speaks to your inner spirit man. In addition, it may inspire you to continue growing closer to the Lord with your spiritual ambition to mature in a special relationship with the Father of Heaven and of Earth.

While I was writing plenty of these thoughts on paper, I believe in my heart without any doubt God used me in a unique way. I Thank God for giving me the ability to share not only my thoughts, but who I am in Christ Jesus to an audience that is on fire for more of his awesomeness to be shared with human mankind in all walks of life.

I have spent ample amounts of time reading books by various authors. I am a woman of high expectations when it comes to my spiritual walk with the Lord. I always feel that God has more of him that I need to know about. At times, I would bury myself in books and study trying to get to the end. Then I realize this is a lifetime process. Everyone who reads likes to read with understanding and get blessed in one way or another. Just like watching a movie or going to see a play, you want to get to the end to see the conclusion. However, I want to get the full understanding of what is going on too.

Believe me when I say this, there are numerous people that need a little more help with reading the bible with understanding. Several who are more fortunate and able to comprehend than others to notice the words of God and go for it. <u>My unique way of writing is out of concern of wanting every soul that reads or hears about this book. I believe God wants to use me to assist him in reaching more people before he returns.</u>

We have to think of our neighbors who love God and want that closer walk with him. Do not get me wrong, I know The Bible says study to show yourself approved. As you continue to seek his face, he will give you the wisdom, knowledge and understanding. As the word of God blesses me, I want to be a blessing to others where maybe the fire has gone out. Possibly they can get back to the basics of <u>Sound Base Doctrine</u>(guideline), which is the word of God. This book can also be encouraging for those who want to have a burning desire to study and build a relationship.

Some of the reading material is deep, but to me that's a challenge. I think it's enjoyable to pull out the dictionary and Concordance to get the understanding of what the author is saying in that <u>first</u> paragraph. (Smile) However, it can be frustrating to spend my reading time seeking research material for the whole book. I do realize some of the Christians and non-Christians who have fallen away, all were not their fault, circumstances that happened out of our control. Like the psalmist says **"We Fall Down, But We Get Up"**. It's just time to rise up above the past circumstance.

We have to take in consideration that we don't want to lose the reader's attention. I have spoken to several people who have gotten aggravated and put the book down and had no desire to complete it. I am going to be real with this next statement. I myself have not completed a few books because of the same situation. Then I have some books I have read all the way through twice. I just do not want to be so inconsiderate and selfish and make the sales and no one gets blessed. I want for them to be so full of God they can't keep it to themselves. Until they have no other choice to tell someone else about the flaming fire of God from someone who has been in their shoes.

My prayer is that everyone with a soul receives the full manifestation of the Holy Spirit in Christ Jesus as Our Lord with the Blessing of God. Obtain his wisdom, knowledge and understanding of the Holy Bible. Take God's word and love him in such a way that not man or nothing could ever come between you and him. Learn his ways in this world and the world to come. Realize that not one can compare to his awesomeness. Keep him in your heart forever and ever.

Amen.

CHARM

LOVE YOU LORD

Introduction

I was not raised in a spiritual setting, but my mother acknowledges God– she believed in his manifestation. So as I got older, I began to see the world in an unpleasant way. Thank God for Grace in Jesus name. God allowed Jesus to come into my life his way. One day I began to read the word of God and didn't understand it, I called myself being the smart-aleck that I was - - I said to God "if you want me to read your word, well give me the understanding", not knowing he would show up! Now the strangest thing was I had not accepted him into my life yet. I hadn't confessed with my mouth but I knew by faith there was a God, somewhere out there.

When I was about 26 years old, I hadn't opened my mouth unto the Lord, I was going on about my business. I remembered something, it was about 3 days later I picked up the word of God and began to read it with **understanding** like never before. That was **exciting** – I was not close to the word but he manifests to me. I felt so ***special***! Don't get me wrong he moved enough to keep me interested in what he had to say. I had to seek him out for myself. He didn't force himself on me; I wanted to know him just as much as he wanted me to get to know him.

A while later, I started going to church. The more I went, the more I enjoyed the word of God. I accepted Christ into my heart. I noticed I didn't handle things the same way, I started to see things differently, and the Peace of God came upon me. A couple of years later, that wasn't enough - - I needed a whole new start on life. So I left the past behind and with the help of the Lord. Pressed my way to a new life, future strength renewed my mind.

I asked God what he would have me to do? What is my purpose? Be careful of questions like that, God will answer. I wanted to be used by God, not by man. Which is better to be used by? Somewhere in our little talks, I started writing my thoughts on paper. Stories, poems, I just gave them out at work or to anyone that may need encouragement. Over a period of time, my notebooks were piling up, sitting in closets or shelves, seminary classes. I asked again, what would you have me to do? Me not paying attention to what people had been mentioning for years – "Why don't you write a book?" I just smiled and said maybe one day when I have time.

Well a few years ago it hit me at 4:30 in the morning, I couldn't go to sleep. Tossing and turning the Spirit spoke and said "Write." I said "write, write what?" You're Not - - What do you mean "You're Not?" I tried to forget this and go back to sleep, but I couldn't sleep until I was obedient to the Spirit. God had the last word, so I got up and started writing about "You're not."

God has inspired me to write different stories, poems in a unique way of expressing his word with understanding for everyone. I thank God for using me in a special way. **Bless his Holy Name.**

Praise for My Vision from God (MVFG)

If you know Charmyne, you would know that she is a person who truly loves the Lord. As her pastor, I have read these memoirs and find that Charmyne writes as she speaks. **To know this is to enjoy it as she allows Jesus flow through her expression.**

Pastor Benjamin W. Mittman
East White Oak Missionary Baptist Church Greensboro, NC

"Must read for the Body of Christ in the Twenty Fist Century". *Sister Charmyne* **brings out in depth points that are eye opening and life changing**. This book is necessary for your library..

Mary Long, Evangelist
Christian Broadcaster for WOKX,
High Point, NC

"I think these writings are **very inspirational** and are **good devotional thoughts.**" Rev. Larry E. Covington Pastor

Ebenezer United Church of Christ Burlington, NC
Burlington, NC

"**Intriguing and inspired by God.** This book is destined to change your life forever". You will never be the same.

Angela Prince-Prophetess
High Point, NC

My Vision From God" is a must read book of spiritual short stories and poems seen through the eyes of the Author, Charmyne Fluker. **She has her own style of writing, best described as straight talk and to the point.**" It was written for and should be enjoyed by all. It will be a blessing to everyone who reads it.

Jacqueline K. Phifer Greensboro, NC

To whoever should read this book, ***blessings will be bestowed upon them.*** This book MVFG is a true inspiration, not only to the <u>Mind and Body, but your</u> **Soul shall prosper** <u>too.</u>

Kenneth L. Hardeman Winston Salem, NC
All Those People

Sometimes we may look at a multitude of people and say "Look at <u>all those people</u>." A large crowd can put fear in you to speak, stutter and stumble over words if you had to speak. They could be very receptive to you or be critical and judgmental towards what you may have to say.

All those people could make you nervous, knowing that their attention is on you. Whether you're speaking, dancing, singing, praising or just acting a plain fool in public or at a restaurant, store etc.

All those people can go along with you or against you and cause tumult (uproar) that may lead to some serious decision making with your own mind: not allowing the crowd to change your beliefs. Just like they did Jesus. (Matthew 27:22-23)

All those people heard of the coming Messiah.

All those people heard and said that a King was born.

All those people saw and experienced his healing and miracles, fed the five thousand, raised the dead, walked on the water, replaced an ear without surgery, saw the lame walk, gave sight to the blind.

All those people were in the synagogue when he taught them, he gave them wisdom, understanding and life.

All those people had received a new revelation.

All those people saw him being arrested after they took counsel. (Advisory Board) Same people decided to free Barabbas and not Jesus.

All those people watch him carry that cross to Calvary.

All those people stood in awe and watched him suffer caring for the sins of the world. All those people heard his cry to the Father, why hath thou forsaken me.

All those people had seen him take his last breath. (John 19:36)

All those people not knowing, but Jesus knowing, these things were done so that the scripture might be fulfilled.

All those people saw after the resurrection, graves were opened and many bodies of the saints, which slept, arose. They went into the city and many appeared into the city. (Matthew 27:52)

All those people that were watching Jesus saw the earthquake and the damage that had taken place they feared greatly and said, "Truly this was the Son of God."

All those people that may have been persuaded to believe the lie that was mentioned in Matthew 28.12-15. The soldiers were paid a large amount of money to say the Christ Disciples stole him. (Vs 15) This lie or saying is commonly reported among the Jews until today.

All those people had seen the resurrected Christ walking the streets of Galilee, who has all power given unto him in heaven and on earth. (Matthew 28:18)

All those people today proclaim to be Christians and are not reading nor studying his word, but all those people attend church religiously Sunday after Sunday.

All those people are missing the full manifestation of God. They are not expecting him to show up.

All those people can stay home, get some rest, save time and gas because they are not waiting with anticipation. (**Just Stay Home**)

All those people need to be expecting to see the move of God, instead some are suspecting. (Doubting)

All those people say they love him and their heart is far away from him.

All those people sit in church every week and will not praise god, will not worship him, and will not raise their hands to give him the glory.

All those people need Christ more than Christ needs them. He will make the rocks cry out Hallelujah if he has to.

All those people in the Church will not talk about or share his awesome power with a sinner to bring them into the knowledge of Christ. Nevertheless, some will talk about his goodness to other Christians. Tell me, why not to the sinners?

All those people deep in their souls know the truth, and they know eventually that change will come. They seem to think they can have God on one side and Satan on the other.

All those people betrayed Jesus then and are still doing it now. God is so merciful he has not released his wrath on all those people. However, if the supposed Christians do not stop acting like the sinners, he will continue sending down unnamable viruses, no name diseases that are spreading like a plague upon the earth. His people will be begging for mercy. Then again you may have some sinners saying, "Look what happened to all those who want to be Christians. They are going to have pity for God's people. Why don't God's people have pity for the lost souls and minister to them.

This time we cannot say it was the family that pierced God's heart. The family of God was Jesus, the beloved son in which he was well pleased. Jesus was a servant to his father and carried out his Father's will, even though it cost him his life. This time the pain that the Creator of the Universe is experiencing is not from the family, it is from **"All those people."**

Jesus

CHARM

ALL THOSE PEOPLE

John the Baptist tried to get all those people prepared,
Knowing that no one else could be compared.
Christ gave knowledge, wisdom and taught God's way,
He wanted them to understand he would die, and rise on the third day.

Born to be a King and Jewish Messiah,
All those people tried to make him out of a liar.

Ignorant to the fact, with his bloodshed, we will be purified,
All those people took council, that he may be crucified.

After he had risen, all those people known as his enemies, pouted,
While believers worshipped, some still yet doubted.

Need not be reminded, Guest we are, Jesus is the Host,
Continue in obedience, teaching and baptizing in the name of
the Father,
Son and Holy Ghost.

                                                    In Jesus Name

                                                    CHARM

There are the faithful and then the unfaithful. Regardless of what everyone else does or I think your decision of faithfulness can make a difference. You can be that faithful person God is looking for. Not like all those people.

CAUGHT UP

Define: Caught – catch: Capture/deceive, Surprise. Catch up to overtake.

Life on Earth can be so fulfilling; enjoying every moment is precious. That is exactly what God would have us do, live a life of abundance. Also remember not to get caught up in or on things of this world. Satan is roaming the earth, with all kinds of distractions to keep you focused on everything but the prize, which is Jesus in heaven.

We can be so into (caught up) various different things in our frequent walks with Christ. We face numerous circumstances daily. The Book of Roman 12:2 says we are not to be conformed to this world but transformed by the receiving of the mind. Meaning changing converting, a new way of thinking. Yes we are in the Land of the Living. We can be in the world without being conformed to the way of the world. Not adjusting to the way Satan wants us to think like him.

For example, some people are caught up on perfection. Let me know who will not make mistakes nor have errors, wrong decisions about something. Christ is the only perfect person that walked God's Green Earth.

Now once you have made a mistake, do not allow pride to get in your way. Get it straightened out, apologizing usually works. Accept that your name has not changed to Jesus Christ, things happen. Confess that you were wrong. Do what need to be done to the person or people, or what the circumstance may be at the time. Now forgive yourself – Isaiah 43:25 I even, I am he that blotted out thy transgressions, for mine own sake and will not remember thy sins. Perfection is something you would want to move towards in Christ Jesus. Allow him to do the work through you that needs to be done. Go forth.

Being caught up in Superstition is another one of those things some people live by. Controlling them to some degree. It's just believing something that has no purpose. If you are steered by the foolishness of superstition then you are ignorant. If you are not careful this junk will dictate you life. Believe what is in the word of God. Do not believe about the Black cats, splitting of a pole, itching hands, etc. If you are living according to that foolishness and not living according to the words of God, something is terribly wrong. Superstition sounds like it is taking control of you. The spirit of God will guide you away from Demonic and controlling forces. "Psalm 32:8 speak of instructing and teaching the way which you shall go. "I will guide you with mine eyes".

Allow the Holy Spirit to dictate or order your steps, not some controlling force that you can't benefit from. Do not let anything separate you from the love of God. Romans 8:38.

We can easily be caught up on so many other things, money – time, religion, music, children, drugs and family activity – TV, life's everyday functions, sports and the list goes on and on.

Caught up on people, relationships - past and present, pastor –other people problems, sad but true caught up on yourself. You get the message.

Do not be so caught up in doing everything, for everybody but Jesus. Numerous things can distract us. Take hold with your attention on the **main attraction Jesus** and grip to it real tight. Get caught up on the Holy Spirit this is what being caught up is all about. God say we are in the the world does not be conformed to the things of the world. If you don't get caught up when Jesus returns – then you will be caught up in the Rapture, which is seven years of tribulation –end times. Being tangled in the wrong thing, then you will have seven years to think about it without the Holy Spirit. The Holy Spirit will not be present in the end times. This world and everything in it will pass away. Now Jesus and his word will stand forever.

Be careful, sometimes you are so caught up and distracted it is pathetic. When you look around the rapture would have come in a twinkle of an eye. The rapture will be a real nightmare, nothing near to TV, so do not be fooled. You still would be concentrating on what you want be caught up for tomorrow. Tomorrow has not been promised to anyone. So do not think you are any better than the next person is. Once rapture comes and you are not caught up on Jesus, well you know the story. Seek out the word of God, find out what's going on. The Book of Daniel, Thessalonians, and Revelation for more understanding, going to bible study at a church that teaches about Jesus Christ as Lord. If not, the other things that you thought was more important than him – will not matter anymore. Three things to think about:

Go forth in your blessings of the Lord

Don't be caught, left behind

Don't be caught Dead or Alive with out him.

Jesus

Charm

CAUGHT UP

JESUS will return in a twinkle of an eye,
Some will and will not ascend to meet him in the sky.

Do not get caught up in things of the world,
Get caught up on diamonds, streets of gold, and pearls.

Get caught up on being rooted, grounded and planting seeds,

Not caught in, trapped doing Satan's deeds.

Do not allow your minds to be minimized,
Get caught up with your eyes on the prize.

Do not get caught up with Satan the Liar,
He is seeking souls to burn with him in the Lake of Fire.

Jesus

CHARM

Basically do not get so involved in life's everyday functions and miss out on the Center of your Joy. <u>Stay focused on the Main Attraction (Jesus).</u>

GET UP AND GO HOME

To some people it's just like a sport, they are out to play the game. Sometimes we want to be recognized well maybe it is not Gods;s time yet. Have you ever thought that he may have to keep you hidden from some people because he has not finished with his masterpiece (supreme artistic achievement)? Some of us want to pretend to perpetuate as if we have it like that. Who are you fooling? "God Knows" if you do and if you don't. The book of Acts beginning with Chapter 4:32 through Chapter 5:1-10 speaks about a husband named Ananias and his wife Sapphira wanting to be recognized and scheme at the same time.

The bible expounds very clearly about playing games with the Lord and lying to get ahead by stealing. God does not take that too likely. They wanted to play, but they picked the wrong person. God used them as an example for everyone to see.

Understand the book of Acts 4 the believers were sharing their possessions, selling land, house, etc. and giving to the Apostles to benefit the church. Therefore, the Apostles were giving it to any one as needed. This husband and wife figured they would get recognition by selling as the believers did but they had something else in mind. Be mindful that the believers were real about their giving. Instead Ananias and Sapphira were not, and God gave them judgement. The game they were trying to play on the Apostles intelligence was to sell a piece of the land, keep a portion and to get all they need from the Apostles. Being ignorant to the fact you can not lie to God. Let it be known they never knew what hit them.

The husband and wife were being secretive (they kept it between them) about selling a piece of property so that they could be recognized for their good deeds before the church. You can't have it all. They allowed Satan to fill their hearts with one lie to many. They sold the goods; they kept part and gave part to the God (Apostles) as if that was all of the money for the price of the land, just as they planned. But they were not smart enough to have a plan B. How many times you know you better have a back-up plan. Things do not always go according to our plan. God has a plan that was predestined. He will have it his way regardless of the outcome

A while later the question was raised to Ananias from Peter, "why did you lie?" Did it belong to you before you sold it and after you sold it? You didn't lie to men, but to God. After he heard Those words he fell down and died. About three hours later his wife came not knowing what had happened to her husband. Peter asked her "is this the price you and your husband got for the land? She replied "yes". Peter asked her "how could you test the spirit of the Lord. Look the the feet of the men who buried your husband are at the door for you. She also fell and died. They buried them together. Fear set in on those who heard. Well today people are doing the same thing thinking they are getting over on God. We need to Thank God repeatedly for Grace and Mercy.

There are people that make very good money and will not give back to God. Minds are so whacked with foolishness. The only reason you have as much as you do is because God made that choice. It's nothing you did that was so worthy. Smiling in church like you are a saint and all the time stealing from God. God despises a hypocrite. Once you start pretending you have to keep it up. A hypocrite just gets dressed on the outside, the inside is dark, sad and ugly. When you begin living double standard you have to keep wearing the mask everywhere you go.

You can continue saying you do not have time and money. That you are too busy to read, study and pray. How do you manage to have time to do everything else you want to do? How is it that you have money to entertain yourself with the things you enjoy? Right about the time you're reading and studying, you're so tired. Come Sunday morning you're sitting on the pews looking around wondering who knows about your little game. Here's that old cliché, which you may know very well. "You can fool some of the people some of the time-some can be fooled most of the time-But you can never Fool God." Playing church to get recognition if you want to be noticed by the people or the people in the church. Your biggest concern is to be noticed by God not by man. Man can not put you in Heaven or in Hell. **If you are one of these people that do not fear God Enough to do the right thing, then you do not fear going to Hell.**

I want you to understand something; God did not kill them only because they lied. They wanted to use the church and take away not to truly give to. You can try to make a fool of God if you want to, he does not have a problem with calling you out too. Just do not set yourself up to be used as an example.

If you are sitting around by Ananias and Sapphira house wanting to see what their next plan is, they do not have any. God has a plan, A, B, C etc in his control, because he is real. Playing church in God's house, there will be judgement for you too. The thing is everyone wants to play, be real with God. You are not happy when you are not real. **God can not use you if you're not real. If you're playing church with Ananias and Sapphira, Get up and Go Home while you are still able.**

God have Mercy on our Souls

CHARM

HUSBAND AND WIFE

They gave the devil room in their hearts to plot a deal,
Not only to lie to God, but also to steal.

That was the last lie to be told by the Husband and Wife,
They had no idea that lying would cost them their life.

When the lies were told, both fell down,
From them you can not hear a sound.

When you are out to play the game,
To play with God's church, it's not the same.

The Bible says they have a place for a thief and a liar,
It is your choice if you end up in the Lake of Fire.

JESUS

CHARM

Do not take from God; give to him you will be blessed. The next time you think about cheating, lying and stealing from God. You had better think twice, because **Hell is Nothing Nice.**

GOD BLESS AMERICA

Our country have always been known as home of the free and the brave,
God bless the parents who visit their young one's grave.
Police was hired to protect us and to serve,
Not to beat us for what they think we deserve.
Cocaine is used for medicine to help relieve the pain,
Now it is on the streets used as Crack Cocaine driving the abusers insane.
Prostitutes used to stand on the corners, now they are dancing on the stage,
It is a pitiful man who does not have a conscience, dancers at thirteen years of age.
God some pastors said you called them, maybe but not to marry ladies and men that are gay.
God I know you do not approve of what is going on at this particular time of day.

God Bless America

You said children are to inherit the earth not pushing up dirt.
You made a new law under Grace and Mercy, that you will give us what we deserve.
You say to be transformed by the renewing of your mind, but minds being corrupt through drug abuse.
Mary Magdalene was a prostitute; Jesus cast out seven demons, and forgave her. We are virtuous women of God.
God you said in the word husbands love your wives, and wives honor your husbands. When God created the earth, he made it clear for man and woman to marry. The Bible says man should not lie with another as if it was a woman.

God Bless America

I merely wrote these few words to let each and everyone realize how much the country is in a desperate need of some serious **Jesus Gangsters.** The wars should resemble the prayer warriors fighting with all that is within them for the glory of God. The flame that we see at the end of a gun that has been fired should have been a release of the flaming Holy Ghost. We have been quenching the spirit and shutting it up in our bones for too long. Knives cutting are the swords of God, working hard, with two edges cutting off the sins of the world. It would be nice if prostitutes were selling the word of god to the sinners at all Four Corners of the world? If people were dancing the David dance only because of the Spirit of the Lord has fell upon them and they can't control themselves.

He will continue sending his angels of protection through the serious Men and Women of God. The comforter has never left from rescuing us if we want to be rescued in a time of need.

If you and I are one of God's people that are hearing the word and not doing the work in the schools or communities, youth centers, walking the pavement. Not doing anything to make this country a better place, then you still want to complain. Most of God's people know who and what exactly I am talking about. (James 1:22 deceiving your own selves)

The precious name you want to proclaim and no action in your deeds then you don't have the right to complain.

In this era, Satan has launched out his attack and they are doing their jobs, look like to the best of their ability. All the round table meetings are nice. However, when you are in battle, who wants to talk? (This means War) Sitting around all the tables in the world can not compare with the true believers of Jesus praying in the Spirit on the same accord.

God Bless America

Bless Your Name Lord

Charm

GOD CHOSE THE SEASON

Allow me to introduce the book of Ecclesiastes, when the seasons of life change. The way I perceived the dissimilar seasons of life in chapter 3:1-8. God is preparing us for all types of situations throughout life. As we look a little closer, the word "time" has several meanings, this particular time meaning "season." This book also reveals to us honestly that God's word faces the world. The book was wrote by David's son King Solomon, the bible called him in Chapter 1:1, words of the Preacher.

Ecclesiastes 3:1-8

1 To Everything there is a season and a time to every purpose under the heaven:
2 A time to be born, a time to die: a time to plant, a time to pluck up which is planted: 3 A time to kill, a time to heal, a time to break down and a time to buildup.
3 A time to weep, and a time to laugh, a time to mourn, and a time to dance.
4 A time to cast away stones, time to gather stones together, a time to embrace, and a time to refrain from embracing.
5 A time to get, a time to lose, a time to keep and a time to castaway.
6 A time to rend and a time to sow, a time to keep silence, and a time to speak. 8 A time to love and a time to hate, a time of war and a time of peace.

God is in control, so why do sometimes we look so distressed? Your facial expression looks as if you have lost your best friend. He is not lost; he is with us through the season as it changes. Occasionally when the season changes it is a little frightening. The period can change from bad to worse or good to better even from bad to good and vice versa.

The Bible says we are going to have trials and tribulations. Meaning, you are not in a fairyland or storybook. Storybook means just that (lying) about life. Romans 5:2 say "we have access by faith into this grace, no matter what's going on or where we are in life, we have the right to enter in faith, no limitations, the ball is in our court. Walk in grace – unmerited favor from God. Romans 5:3 say, "we glory in tribulations". Tribulations worketh patience. We are to carry our joy and triumph into the midst of our trials.

Phil 1:20 Through trials and tribulations, Christ should be magnified in the body whether it be by life or by death. So whatever season you are in we are to give Glory to God knowing by faith it's going to be alright. Not because of what our eyes can see; but by trusting and believing in God. He knows this strengthens us, builds us, mold us to the way he wants us to be. Our life on this earth is very much real-problems, situations, circumstances, tears, pain, sorrow, healing, happiness, emotional and physical. The minds are being poisoned with lies, alcohol, drugs, and prostitution. <u>Some carnal minds would see it, as that's just the way it is. It can be</u> true if you allow it to sink into the depth of your soul. Then again, it can also be another lie, which is what Satan wants you to believe.

God knew about before hand these things. God has the knowledge, he is already aware of what taking place in our lives. He also fixed it, for that season only. You do not have to take it lying down. You can fight if you choose to. Just like God has chose the season, then you can chose to trust and believe in him. You cannot fight lying down anyway. Furthermore, you can fight on your knees.

Now as the season has changed from winter to spring, your season in life can change also. Maybe, just for a little while. Well your season could possibly be that you feel you can have church at home every Sunday. If a church that you are attending is not functioning to your satisfaction, do you think that is a reason to fall away from all churches? Always have a season to continue on to get a word from the Lord. You very well might just be having a rough time and has fallen away from prayer. A change in your attitude toward everyday life situations can mess your mind up. If our attitude has changed, we would like to think it is the other people with the problem. Now if this begins to happen frequently, stand back and look in the mirror. If may be you. There are times we do not understand God. <u>The question may arise why is this happening to</u>

me. Believe me when I say this, all of us have difficulties as we go through life. You may have a situation that you handle better than I, or vice versa. Nevertheless, give it to Jesus, he handles all of our problems. All of God's people have a testimony. It' s not just you. **Please just don't give up on God. He has a way of working things out.**

Although the season of life has changed for us, we need to know Jesus Christ doesn't. He is the same today, yesterday and forever. (Hebrew 13:8) This is your season now to realize God knows what we are going through. He knows who will accept him, and who will reject him. Who will rebel against him? Whom he will be able to trust? Who put all their trust in him? Who will be strong enough to stand on the front line? Who will continue to love him when things don't go their way? God is all knowing (omniscience). God has unlimited authority (omnipotence). He know if your season has changed for better or for the worst.

Be encouraged in his word, God has the power to change all things if it is his will through prayer. Watch and pray you can see it coming if you are willing to yield to the Holy Spirit. Each trial, each tribulation, each season God has it all under control. Now let us stop limiting God's power. We may say with our mouth and maybe believe in our hearts, but still limit God's authority. The season is here and now, for us to trust in God. Glorify him in and out of season, for every thing there is a reason. Praise him for what he is doing, for what he has done, and for what he is about to do. Allow the fruit of his words to be upon your lips continually.

Another season has come and gone. Another one is on the way. This is your season to serve. Remember **"God Chose the season."**

Glory, Glory, Glory

CHARM

GOD CHOSE THE SEASON

To live life to the fullest in God's sight, That you may be able to sit at the right.

We may ask the question or if there's a reason, To everything, there is a season.

When you have tears of sadness or tears of sorrow, Look up to Jesus to give you a brighter tomorrow.

Peace comes to mind when I see a dove, Prayer comes to mind when I think of God's love.

Jesus

CHARM

I NEVER DONE NOTHING WRONG

There are people that have been born and grown up in the church all their lives. Maybe they have never done anything wrong as our eyes can see. The bible says in Matthew 9:13-<u>He has not come to call the righteous, but sinners to repentance.</u> (KJV)

Pharisee saw Jesus Christ with the Publicans and Sinners and they did not understand. Jesus goes where he sees there is a need at the time, if you are not sick; there is no need for a physician. He feels it is proper that he should associate with them for the purpose of doing them good. No human being by nature is righteous.

If you just continue being patient with me for a little while you then can understand Romans 3:9-18 (King James Version)

NONE IS RIGHTEOUS

Vs 9- What then? Are we better than them? No, in no wise: for we have before proved both Jews and Gentiles that they are all under sin:
Jews have no advantage over the Gentiles, both failed to keep the law; they are Sinners.

Vs 10- As it is written, "There is none righteous, no not one:"
Both failed and equally dependent on the mercy of God. Incapable of justified and saved by their works.

Vs 11-There is none that understandeth, there is none that seeketh after God.
By God being the searcher of hearts, none that understood him or wise enough to serve or obey him. None seek to know or do his will. Not to seek after him is neglect.

Vs 12- They are all gone out of the way, they are together becoming unprofitable: there is none that doeth good, no, not one.
They have declined for the path of piety (religious) and virtue (pure). They are as one joined; they have no value about the works of righteousness.

Vs 13- Their throat is an open sepulchre; with their tongues they have use deceit; the poison asps in under their lips:
This is like an open grave to all that receive into the (destruction) slander. If not careful, it will swallow up the peace and happiness of others. With their tongues they have been false and unfaithful to people. Under their lips is poison as in wicked men spreading words of slander quickly destroying the reputation and happiness of man.

Vs 14- Whose mouth is full of cursing and bitterness:
David is describing his bitter enemies. Cursing is disgraceful language, cruelty and malicious words.

Vs 15- Their feet are swift to shed blood:
Eagerness of the nation to commit crime. They thirsted for the blood of innocence and haste (quick) to shed it.

Vs16- **Destruction and misery are in their ways:**
The tendency of their conduct is to destroy the virtue (pure) happiness and peace of all people meet.

Vs 17- And the way of peace they have not known:
Their main purpose is plans of evil. Do not know and regard (respect) to promote the welfare of themselves or others. This is a case of selfishness and seeks to gain for their purposes of crime and ambition.

Vs 18- There is no fear of God before their eyes.
The only thing that is effectual (result) in restraining men from sin will be a regard (fear-reverence-awe) to the honor and law of God.

Just do not be so ignorant to think that you have it made because you treat people with respect. Ok, you trimmed the old lady bushes in her yard every now and then. Some people may even keep up with the favors that they do for other people. <u>It is good to be kind toothers.</u> Well say you are the one that never done nothing-wrong person. People have always spoken well of you,and you feel to believe that you have it all together. The truth is you have really fallen apart. You have deceived yourself. (I John 1: 7-10) (KJV **(vs 7)** " But if we walk in the light, we have fellowship one with another, and the blood of Jesus Christ his(God) son cleanseth us from all sin. **(Vs 8)** If we say that we have no sin, **we deceive ourselves, and the truth is not in us.** (Vs 9) If we confess our sin, he is faithful and just (righteous) to forgive us our sins and to cleanse us for all unrighteousness. (Vs 10) If we say that we have not sinned, we make him a liar, and his word is not in us." You the nice person who is righteous, have you confess Jesus as your Lord and Savior. Romans 10:9 "That if thou shalt confess with thy mouth the Lord Jesus and shalt believe in thine heart that God hath raised him from the dead and thou shalt be saved."

Jesus has made it so uncomplicated for us to accept him to be saved: **Mark 16:**16 says he that believeth it and is baptized shall be saved: But he that believeth not shall be damned.

Aunt Alice, Mary, Brittany, Uncle Joe Etc…They have a lot of nice, good-hearted people in the world that do not mind doing things to help out. Even the generous people that are always seeking to work with the shelters, feed the homeless, visit the nursing homes, not cursing when elderly is present, giving money for different causes or charities. Before any one of these good,honest hard working folks leave this earth, the question should be asked sooner or later "Are they Saved?"

I asked you if you do know some people that you have become acquainted with, find out before it's too late. They may be ashamed to talk about the Lord, but you my Christian friends should be able to speak out boldly to the lost souls. God's way should be taught by you to all souls. Our good deeds will never equal up to righteousness in God's sight. Isaiah 64:6 says "But we are all as an unclean thing and all our righteousnesses (deeds) are as filthy rags." (KJV)

If you have never done anything wrong, then something is drastically wrong. *All of us were born sinners. Jesus is the only one that has never sinned.* You need to get in touch with God, with yourself and with others. **This is for those who have never fell short of the Glory of God; well you are not saved.**

This is something I believe may help you understand **Righteous**.

1. Righteous is right standing with God. Standing in the presence of God without feeling guilt.
2. Righteous by Faith is available to all that believe the declaration.
3. Righteous declaration is being Born Again, God declared you are righteous.
4. Righteous are your Rights to be free from Sin.

They have plenty of Good Hearted people in Hell. Then again, could be more Church Attendees in Hell with the Good Hearted Folks.

Only God Knows…

In The Name of Jesus

CHARMt

I NEVER DONE NOTHING WRONG

This is for a believer of God, but a non-believer thinking they have never done nothing wrong.

I have been born and raised in church all my life,
I don't hate, envy or walk in strife.

I don't drink alcohol, wine or gin,
Therefore my brother I walk without sin.

I don't hangout in clubs, gamble or smoke,
When Jesus comes back, I'm not afraid, I won't have to choke.

See you all need to get your acts together,
Jesus is coming and I am going to continue doing better

Time is passing quickly, and it won't be long,
I have done so well, I sing, I never did nothing wrong.

I don't call psychics, read astrology or do witchcraft,
I'm not weary of Satan's list that he has drafted.

I don't hangout with bums and thugs,
Therefore, you need to know I don't do drugs.

I never lied, stole or cheated,
I will be at the right with Jesus while he is seated.

People would like to think I'm insane,
Because I'm not known to fuss and complain.

As I said before, it won't be long,
I will continue singing my beautiful song,
I'm one of those who have never done nothing wrong.

JESUS

CHARM

They really have beautiful spirits; good generous people that we know or come in contact frequently. We sometimes may feel they are so good, have we ever thought because they are so nice but *"Are they saved"?*

PERFECT PEACE

God wants to give you peace, not ordinary Peace, His Perfect Peace. While you are in a storm, he says my peace. The calmness of his peace you shall have through the word of God.

God has spoken perfect peace to situations and circumstances for his people

Why were the men so frightened?

Here are a few reasons why God wants us to receive his perfect peace.

1. You should not be lacking in nothing-faith.
2. If you lack wisdom ask God in faith.
3. Believe that God wants us to ask of him anything in faith and it will be given to us.
4. Knowing this of your faith worketh patience.
5. Show me thy faith without work and I will show they my works-faith without works is dead.

You have to trust in God totally.

He expects us to lack in nothing and trust in him with everything.

Trust in God with all thine heart.

Many people claim to believe in him, still yet will not trust in him.
Only to say they're going by what they see with their physical eyes, not God's spiritual eyes.
I Tim 4:10 Says trust in the living God who is the Savior of all men.
Trust in a friend is one thing, but to know that you know.
Believe that you believe, Jesus is the one and; only one you should be trusting. Trusting God with everything and remembering that promises are being fulfilled.
Eph. 6:2 First commandment with promise shall be fulfilled if you believe in the living word of God.

II Tim 1:2-Promises of life in Christ Jesus. **Heb 10:22** for he is faithful that promised.

People trust man promises, but promise of life through Jesus Christ, some just don't believe.

We trust man everyday when we go to work. Have faith that man is going to have our paycheck on payday, but have a problem with God promises. Remember promises are being fulfilled through Christ Jesus according to your faith.

Phil 4:7 He will give you peace that passeth understanding, while you are going through trials and tribulations. You can still have peace.

When the peace of God rest upon you, no one would ever know you were going through a storm or have been through a storm.

John 14:27 Jesus says peace I leave with you. My peace I give you.

1. He's going to leave it with you.
2. He's going to give it to you, my peace. He owns peace just like he owns everything else.

Then he said let not your heart be troubled or afraid. You have a friend that would never leave you. He gave it all.

While they were in the boat, water swamped over the sides you really believe you are sinking and about to die. **Fear** set in first, then panic. Just as the disciples did when Jesus took them to the other side of the Sea of Galilee. Other boats were with them on that particular day. A great windstorm (tempest) came about, billow beating on the side of the boat; begin to fast filling with water. Jesus was in the back of the boat probably had a long day, resting himself. Not bothering anyone, but they didn't feel the same about bothering him. He was catching him some Z-Z-Z-S. Until they came waking him up talking about this windstorm.

That storm would have come whether Jesus was on the boat or not. I believe Jesus stood back and looked at them with sleep in his eyes. Ask them, **where is your faith**? None of them could answer. All of them together wouldn't do a thing. <u>They were too afraid to know to have peace in the midst of a storm.</u>

In other words they were worrying about the wrong thing. Just like we do now. *They should have been wondering, what the Lord is going to do if they wake him up with that foolishness?*

Just like our kids, they wake us up for anything, I mean anything. You and I know it don't make any sense. Most of the time we give them what they want just to shut them up, and to get them out of our face. <u>Jesus may have felt something about that thing. Maybe he said Peace be still, now go to bed.</u>

Jesus said I have not given you the spirit of fear, but love, peace and sound mind. That fear and panic was not of God. Come to think about it, <u>the disciples never did answer where their faith</u> was. But we know they didn't have any.

When Jesus said, **Peace Be Still**. You can just feel the calmness. Disciple's mouths and eyes were wide open. They didn't know what to think. Maybe glazed at him as he walked away to going about his business. To finish getting his sleep on. <u>Questioning, one to another,</u> **"What manner of man is this, that even the wind and the sea obey him?"** Do they not know this is the Son of Man .Just speak ---- it's done. The men were in the boat with the Lord physically and still yet were afraid, just as we are today in the arms of the Lord.

Your storm can be a number of circumstances or situations. It can be sickness, alcohol or have a bad relationship, in or out the home, unsaved loved ones. Pray about it, let go and let God. He will give you peace in the midst of the storm. Trust that God bought you in it and he'll bring you out.

I have heard a saying sink or swim. Sink you die/swim you fight to stay on top, with the peace that the Lord has given to you.

Lacking nothing. Trusting God with everything. Believing in the fulfillment of his promises. It's impossible for him to lie. He gives peace that passeth understanding.

When the Storm of Life is Raging make sure your soul is anchored in the Lord Jesus Christ. He is not only the way maker...**HE IS THE WAY**.

JESUS

CHARM

PERFECT PEACE

In the beginning god spoke things into existence,
There was no limited distance.

Jesus is one in trinity,
God, Jesus, Holy Spirit is one in unity.

Jesus decided to take a ride, And sail to the other side.
While they were sailing,
Windstorm swept down, faith started failing.

Hearts and minds were pondering---danger,
Not remembering the man in the boat was born in a manger.

His body was at rest,
He managed to awake at his best.

He spoke to the wind and the raging waves,
He's the same today, still yet saves.

Question of faith asked, while the men were afraid,
Amazed in a silent daze.

One to another, "what manner of man is this?
Commands the wind and the water, they don't attempt to resist.

JESUS

CHARM

JESUS CALMS A STORM

In the beginning god spoke things into existence,
There was no limited distance.

Jesus is one in trinity,
God, Jesus, Holy Spirit is one in unity.

Jesus decided to take a ride,
And sail to the other side.

While they were sailing,
Windstorm swept down, faith started failing.

Hearts and minds were pondering---danger,
Not remembering the man in the boat was born in a manger.

His body was at rest,
He managed to awake at his best.

He spoke to the wind and the raging waves,
He's the same today, still yet saves.

Question of faith asked, while the men were afraid,
Amazed in a silent daze.

One to another, "what manner of man is this?
Commands the wind and the water, they don't attempt to resist.

JESUS

CHARM

This writing is not only about having **faith and peace**, it is also about **obedience**. Why is that everything God has created is more obedient than Human Mankind?

THE BEAUTY OF PRAISE AND WORSHIP

Psalms 150 explains how we are to praise the Lord.

Praise in his sanctuary, firmament (expanse, fullness) of his power, praise his mighty acts (deeds), according to his excellent (surpassing) greatness. Praise him with sound of trumpet (lute), and harp, with timbrel (tambourine), dance, stringed instruments and organs (pipe). Praise him upon high loud (clanging) cymbals, and praise him upon high cymbals (loud clashing). Let everything that has breath Praise the Lord. Praise ye the Lord.

Exalt him with dignity. Here in Philipians 4:8 expounds that which are true, honest, just, pure, lovely, and of good report. If there be any virtue (principle of right conduct), if there be any praise "Think on these things." When you think on these things, your mind and spirit are with joy. Your feelings may be exalted in your mind and spirit as you begin to praise the Lord. Praise is merely saying Good Things. Everything about God is Good. God is all of that and some. We can't say enough about the goodness of God. We can also be so excited about him until words cannot explain his excellence. The gladness that you feel can capture you because of his worthiness.

Worship God in Spirit and in Truth. John 4:23 speaks of the true worshipers. Some people are going through the motions. The true worshipers are worshiping from the heart with intense love for God. I want you to understand, they know the spirit by the faith perspective and don't have to see him, and they just know that they know. Philippians 3:3 say we worship God in spirit and rejoice in Christ without confidence in the flesh. John 1:17 said the law came by Moses and, grace and truth came by Jesus Christ. (Romans 5:1) (Paraphrase) **There is one man, one death, one Christ; there is only one truth.) Show God by not being ashamed** of him with fear of raising hands, thank God for your hands, some people do not have hands to raise. You are not ashamed of a blessing are you? How can you be ashamed of the reality of a blessing? The only reason or purpose we are here is to praise and worship the living God. Believing in God's son Jesus and trusting in the Holy Spirit is knowledge.

Admiring him for his goodness and forgetting about us. Allow the spirit and mind to be set free to worship.

The beauty of Praise and Worship is simply not caring about who is looking, or what they are saying. If your mind, spirit and heart were focus on him and his greatness, you would not have time to see what others are doing. Nor how they are praising and worshipping God. The beauty of it all is saying all the good things about him and showing him by worshipping him in admiration. Continually allow the praise of the Lord thy God be upon they lips.

Praise God in Song and Stand – II Chronicles 20:19

And the Levites and of the children of the Kohathites, and the children of the Korhites, stood up to praise the Lord God of Israel with a loud voice on high

Praise with the clapping of the hands – Psalm 47:1
Shout unto God with the voice of triumph. The Clapping and Shouting the victory is won.

Bless the Lord now by being able to lift your hands.
Thus will I bless thee while I live; I will lift up my hands in thy name. (Psalm 63:4)

Lift your hands in the Sanctuary and Bless the Lord. (Psalm 134:1)
I will therefore pray that men everywhere lift up holy hands. (I Timothy 2:8)

Praise God by opening your mouth. (Audible)

I will bless the Lord at all times: His praise shall continually be in my mouth. (Psalm 34:1)

And when they heard that, they lifted up their voice to God with one accord. (Acts 4:24)

Bless the Lord O my soul: and all that is within me, bless his Holy Name. (Psalm 103:1)

JESUS

CHARM

THE BEAUTY OF PRAISE AND WORSHIP

The beauty of praise is not only from the lips, but also from the heart,
Not allowing circumstances to change you or to depart.

Praise and Worship is your inner being crying out, Soul, mind and spirit joined without a doubt.

Give God the glory, honor and the praise, It is ok for your voice to be raised.

Praise him while you are still young with youth, Worship him in spirit and in truth.

Praise him with mind, body, and soul, Worship him while your body is feeble and old.

When Jesus back was against the wall,
The Beauty is he cared enough to pay for us all.

Hallelujah

JESUS

CHARM

THE TABLE IS SET

John 14:2 Jesus said in my father's house are many mansions: If it were not so, I would have told you. I'll go to prepare a place for you.

You know what a house represents- "a building where you take on residence-you live there." Let your mind goes for a little while. Think of the word many meaning numerous or large number, then the word mansion meaning large resident.

Just inside God's house are many mansions. There are enough large residents for any and every one that truly wants one. Remind yourself that in the spiritual realm of God you can't compare his mansions to the ones on this earth.

John 14:6 says "I am the way the truth and the life. No man cometh to the father but by me. The word "But" meaning Only through Jesus you can see the father, which is God. You can't see

God's Kingdom without believing in Jesus as the Son, God as the Father and the Holy Spirit as the Comforter, John 14:16. The Comforter which the father will send in my name, John 14:26.

Book of Revelations 21:2 speaks of the Holy City. John saw the holy city New Jerusalem coming down out of heaven, prepared. Just the way Jesus said he was going to do in John 14:2 about preparing a place. Jesus is not going to arrange a ghetto setting for the righteous that is for sure. He went to get the kingdom ready for the righteous, the righteous will see God, and shall reign forever and ever (never ending-living eternally, never dying) with God.

We see pictures of advertisements all the time saying "just like paradise". Paradise suppose to be a beautiful place. Beautiful clear water, relaxing, and not a care in the world. The place that Jesus went to prepare will blow your natural mind trying to picture it. Your spirit will just go off to think of a place where God will wipe away your tears, no death, no sorrow, and no pain. Revelation 21:18-27 & 22:1-4.

When you enter into the gates made with pearls, and the wall was made of jasper. The foundations of the city were garnished with beautiful, twelve different precious stones. We call them birthstones. The city was gold; the street was made of gold that was transparent as glass.

The shining light is the Glory of God. Will not have any more nights, midst of the street a river on both sides with the tree of life. The throne of God, the Lamb and the servants shall serve him, and live forever.

Revelation 22:17 (AMP) said the word come three times. "The spirit and the bride (the church, true believers), say **, Come.** And let the one who hearth (listening) say, **Come.** And let the one ho is thirsty, **Come;** let the ones who wishes take drink the water of life without cost (freely). " This is Jesus' invitation to accept him, because he will surely come quickly. All three times when he says the word **come** is an invitation to receive him, hear him, accept him and believe that he is the Lord and Savior of this world and the world to come.

He has invited you to live with him forever in the many mansions; he said you shall live and never die. <u>Be honest, who wants to die? Dying is of Ok if you're going to be with Christ.</u>

There are some people whose spirits are dead and walking on the earth. By the way, that is called the walking dead. When you drink this water, you shall never thirst again. When are you going to realize that Christ is not hanging on the cross and is alive? <u>Just accept who he is.</u>

I am sure people in this world have invited you to dinner or places you had no business going and you accepted. Did that stop you? No and you thought you were having such a good time.

Now he has offered you to receive him, that you may have more than this world could ever give you, and you turned him down cold.

Out of all that, he is still allowing you another chance to live in a real mansion eternally.

YOU MAKE THE CALL.
Here are some simple instructions to follow to get into the mansion.

Repent - Turn away from sin and follow God.
Believe - Trust in Jesus.
Confess - Acknowledge Jesus – Romans 10:9.
Call - ask him for forgiveness, eternal life and hope.

We all need some spiritual food, take one day at a time, and one step at a time. In order to visualize the Kingdom of God you have to seek Jesus first. He has come to you more than once in a lifetime; he has given you a personal invitation to the Kingdom, with his arms open to greet you. R. S.V.P. let him know you are coming through repenting, believing, confessing, calling on him, and we do not want to leave out all your good deeds.

Open your heart to receive him. He has prepared the way. Jesus is waiting on you.

THE TABLE IS SET

He has called you by name,
To let it be known he is the same.

He allowed the thunder to roar,
When he knocked at your heart's door.

Without any regrets,
He's prepared, the table is set.

CHARM

JESUS

UNCONDITIONAL LOVE

Love: Strong compassionate affection.
Unconditional: un– not, conditional-existing state-change or altar, absolute without stipulation-without requirements.

Christ will not change his love for us regardless of the existing state we are in, he loves us.

<u>Love can be many things</u>; it can be splendid, imposing, and impressive in size. It can definitely be beautiful. Love also may be expressed in many kinds of ways; you can show love through gifts, hugs and kisses. We cannot leave out emotions, when your feelings take total control, even when we did not want it to. Do you think this may be one of those games where the not so sincere person does things that touches the heart of a person that is not playing a game at all.

Could it be just out of our love for them we are expecting them to feel the same. What about the ones that try to impress that person to make them think you love them, and lead them astray.

<u>Love can be an infatuation</u>, to have foolish passion obsession (doing stupid stuff). In other words, you may play a role of a fool. Everyone has done silly things. Nevertheless, why continue doing them. However, you say, that's love, seems to be more infatuation than love. However, if you call that love---Okay.

Love can last for a season just as well, as for a lifetime. Some people have a way of saying I love you. Then again, some have difficulty saying I love you. Maybe even I love you if you love me. The word love sometimes can be used too loosely, like the want to be players of this world that play simple childish games with the word "Love". How much do you love me? That was a question that Jesus asked Peter, just after he denied him. Of course Peter replied I love you. The way Peter said it did not convince Jesus. The world speaks of the word love so freely and thinks nothing about. What kind of Love Jesus was replying to? Agape love (<u>brotherly</u>) is the love he wanted to hear in Peter's voice. Would you die for me? Maybe you are one that says I love you if you love me. <u>What if I do not</u>

love you; will you still love me? The truth of the matter is that the *correct answer is supposed to be yes.* The flesh will say no. Just for the records to love one another is a commandment from God. Love can be conditional or unconditional. Thank God, Christ loves us unconditional, meaning that regardless of our sinful nature he manages to forgive and forget.

Love can be lost; like each, one of us lost our first love. He has to be first, simply because he loved us before we even came into the knowledge of knowing who he was. Some seek out love and never find it. Some people love the idea of being in love. **Love never loved anybody**.

He loved us from the beginning of the world. I wonder what happens to the certain percentage that seeks out love and never finds it. Could that possibly be the bitter, jealous folk? Then there is the percentage that looks for love in all the wrong places. Genuine love usually not found in clubhouses, drug and sex parties in hotels, *trying to make love out of nothing.* You cannot make someone love you. This should be a natural process with time as the factor. **Allow you to be yourself and let them love you for who you are**. Either they love you or they just don't.

A songwriter once asked a question **"What love have to do with it?"** If you think on that level, I guess nothing. Christ Says Love is the Greatest, so **Love is Everything.** *You do not have to sell yourself cheap for love when the love of God is Rich as it gets.*

Loving the idea of being in Love and not getting love in return or not giving love can be devastating to someone who is a caring person giving their all. This is a give and take world, because when you are giving, someone is always there to receive, be careful. Having a giving heart is a blessing from God. When Jesus is in the mist of giving there is nothing to it.

The subject, Love can also be like a well-very deep. John 3:16 God so loved the world he gave his only begotten son. He loved this world more than anything. He gave up a lot to mankind, more than we could ever give. God presented his love, and released his only son to this world.

Some of us have given up on our families, our children and friends to this world. Christ came not to condemn the world but that the world may be saved through him. Christ suffering was not in vain, why are you giving your children to the world of Satan, who doesn't love anybody but himself. You have a gift from God almighty. Cherished gifts are precious.

People can have the craziest explanations why they love and why they don't love. Then again, some hate more than they love. I believe they have people that love to hate. Majority of the <u>player haters</u> does not have a clue to why they feel that way. The love of God needs embedding into your spirit through Jesus Christ. The agape Love is what Christ is expecting from his people. As long as you are on God's green earth, and talking about whom you hate, you are hindering your blessings. Stop thinking of excuses and reasons why it is so hard for you to love your enemy (Matthew 5:44). I have heard some people say that they truly **Hate** someone.

Hate is a harsh word. Christ loves you as messed up as you are; <u>you can change that</u> **nasty attitude** <u>with the help of the Lord.</u> You may not like them or how they conduct themselves. Pray for them and learn to love them from a distance (Smile), and it will be alright.

You have to be prudent (careful): the choice of words can be vandalistic (destroying) to someone. Words can be very powerful, then again, you do not know the future, and you may need that person you said you hate. If you have room in your heart to hate, you couldn't possibly have room for Jesus. Jesus is Love. Matthew 15:11 Says we are defiled (sully-spot stain-dirty) for which come out the mouth of man. Permit love to come out of your mouth, not hatred. When Jesus Christ lives in your heart, you do not have time to <u>hate nothing but sin.</u> Matthew 6:24 says you cannot serve two masters; you will love one and hate the other.

Love can be hard and tough.
Love can be soft and sweet.
Love can be amiss (loving someone for the wrong reason.)
Love can bring you together or it can tear you apart.
I will repeat that love can be many things.

Before you can love anything or anybody, **you need to fall in love with yourself.** If you don't love yourself, how in the world can you love another? Jesus would love you to love him and keep his commandments. Once you have gotten to this point, meaning filled with the love of Jesus in your heart you will have so much love, enough to make you think you're going to burst.

Plenty of love for family, friends, and even for your enemies. **Thank God.** This can only happen with the love of Christ, which is a compassionate unconditional love. Jesus has splendid love for us without terms. That sounds like music to my ears.

The bible could not have deliberated the love of God for us through his seed Jesus Christ any better to me than in John 15:13 "great love hath no man than, that a man lay down his life for his friends. *(Question)* Do you know any friends that would die for you? We know what **they say** they will do. I will answer the question for some of you, "NO." As for that matter "what about family members willing to die for you?" Well while you are thinking about the answer to the question, allow me to inform you about a friend that has shared all the promises of what God has told him. He has made it known to us. Jesus did not keep <u>Secrets</u> from us about the Love he has for the children of God. <u>The promises that have been made that can't be broken, simply because it is impossible for him to lie.</u>(Hebrew 6:18) He promises always to be with us until the end. He will stick closer than any brother will. You could not find a better friend than Jesus even if you search the whole earth.

<u>Love can be tough and hard</u>. God disciplines us. I believe God shows us tough Love that is why we are becoming better, stronger individuals. In addition, we are building character, along the way picking up his ways. So just for the record, it is OK to discipline your children. The bible speaks about in Proverbs 3:12 "for whom the Lord loveth he correcteth; even as a father the son in whom he delighteth." Proverbs 13:24 says" He that spareth his rod hateth his son: but he that loveth he chasteneth him betimes (seasonably). This is a clear statement. God chastises us because we are his children, so we chastise our children when they are wrong and need correction for wrongdoings. God trains us the way he would have us to go, his way. He started out training us early in our Christian walk although some of us were hard headed. He will get his way before it is all over. We should train our children starting in early childhood.

Love can be soft and sweet. That love gives you comfort while you are going through the valley. I know you did not **stop** in the valley because, the bible says Psalm 23:4 "though I walk through the valley". We all are over comers of the world because Jesus said so in John 16:33. I am talking about that soft love, when the peace of God rest in your heart, no matter what foolishness man or the stupid devil is talking about it will not intimidate (worry) you. Just by trusting him, you feel in your spirit that everything is going to be alright. You know that soft love when he whispers in your ear and you recognize the voice that says, "thus saith the Lord has spoken" about his promises that he cannot break. Yea I am talking about that soft love. The kind of soft Love that will have our hearts melting like butter in a microwave. Something about that, Jesus and I love it.

Corinthians 2:14-15 expounds about sweet savour in a way that will make you want to know more about Christ. (Verse 14) Now thanks be unto God, which always causeth us to triumph in Christ, I and maketh manifest the savour of his knowledge by us in every place. (Verse 15) For we are unto him God a sweet savour of Christ, in them that are saved, and in them that perish: (saved for them accept Christ) (perish for those that reject Christ).

As we labor for God and win the victories, the fragrance that we get comes from knowing him. Being led by Christ is acceptable to God. The sweet incense is for them that have the saviour by accepting Christ into your life. This is well pleasing to God. We are grateful to God, but he is saying that accepting Christ, we have the aroma of Christ. In addition, we talk about his pleasant smelling fragrance. He wants us to have it. Now that is mighty sweet of him.

Love can be amiss. In Love or Loving someone for the wrong reason can be painful, physically, mentally, emotionally or spiritually. In case you don't understand, let me say, **the more they have (material things or money), the more you love them** (that is sorry and is not cool). You and I know that is not genuine Love. Then again they have people out here that have their own motives of <u>why</u> they love a person. In other words, He hits me <u>but he's</u> all I have and a good provider. Some could be financial gain that they feel are beneficial to them. In the long run we know how it usually turns out. Not only a few single parents, men or women seeking out relationships for help with the kids. This day and time men are seeking help where women have left him with the children. <u>Certain motives people have may not be as genuine as others may believe.</u>

Selfish motives I believe are the one that bother me the most. When they want to come in the relationship begging, always looking for something in return for everything they do. Probably racking their little brains out trying to see how they can benefit from this relationship. People are so **seriously stuck on material** things, such as nice houses, cars, well paying jobs, money in the bank, your credit cards, etc. Do not get me wrong you are supposed to want and have the best out of life, and to prosper. I hope the person that you do have a relationship with has something going for him or her. However, you can not just enter the relationship with your big eyes, and your hand out expecting. They have other credentials you may need to look into first. Check to see if you even **like the person as a person, instead of forcing yourself to adjust to their belongings.** <u>**Stuck on a Life of Material things can lead to a Life of Misery.**</u> Everything that people have accomplished in life, some have worked very hard. All was not just given to them, some suffered dearly. It is pathetic when you love them for what they have or what they have to give you.

When you meet someone, Whatever happens to "Are you saved? What church do you attend?

What time is bible study at your church? <u>I Guess Things Got in the Way.</u>

<u>**Love can bring you together or tear you apart.**</u> I think about Samson and Delilah when it comes to the point of being together or being apart. When Samson had met Delilah and Lust and Love is what entangled him. The man forgot all about the vow as a Nazarite. He began playing with her about where his strength comes from. Three times, he teased her, and gave in to her on the fourth time after she had been nagging him about it daily. He had to love her to share that part of his heart with her. Maybe he figured they were going to be together in the future and put

his trust in her. His innermost secrets that he shared with her turned into a nightmare. Later when he fell asleep, Delilah had his head shaved; now he is just like any other man. She was in love, but not with Samson, the eleven hundred pieces of silver was more to her liking. Samson sharing his secret may have wanted the love that brings you together. Delilah has the kind of love that would tear you apart and do not care. You can love someone too much and not enough love. This friend will definitely tear you apart.

True love conquers all.
Love has qualities –negative and positive.
Love does not suppose to change when you are wrong.
Real love never fails.
The powers that love have.

There are several kinds of love. Only One God and One Devil. Satan wants any soul that will come whether you are young or old. He will deceive us so you know how he would poison a young child who is not strong enough to fight; they need covering under the blood. It is up to us to pray for and over our children; Satan's influence is nothing nice. God has put us first, now why we cannot do the same for him. He has proved his love repeatedly and still manifesting since day one. He gave to mankind what was most important to him. If you can do the same, you need to prove your love and show him your gratification. Come on now, your only Son to this World. *Now That's God*. Jesus is Love. Love is one of the greatest gifts. (I Corinthians 13:13) Regardless of whom you are what you have done, and what you are doing. God is a forgiving God. (Matthew 12:31-32)

THE GIFT OF LOVE

If I speak in tongues of mortals and of angels, but do not have love, I am a noisy gong or a clanging cymbal.

If I have prophetic powers, and understand all mysteries and all knowledge, and if I have all faith, so as to remove mountains, but do not have love, I am nothing.

If I give away all my possessions, and if I hand over my body so that I may boast, but do not have love, I gain nothing.

Love is patient; love is kind; love is not envious or boastful or arrogant or rude.

It does not insist on its own way; it is not irritable or resentful; it does not rejoice in wrongdoing, but rejoices in the truth. It bears all things, believes all things, hopes all things, endures all things.

Love never ends. (I Corinthians 13:1-8)

JESUS love is a perfecting bond of unity.

In Jesus Name

CHARM

UNCONDITIONAL LOVE

The love I share is like no other,
I promised to stick closer than any brother.

Regardless of all your mistakes and faults,
Not counting all the people you hurt with them ugly insults.

I love you with your unpleasant conditions,
I'm sitting at the right with your petitions.

Yes I see your gifts and spiritual sight,
But it's my joy and spiritual might.

I love you enough to lend you a helping hand
Now with my strength you can withstand.

The love I give you to share,
Only heaven above knows how much I care.

Your heart should be pure and sacred,
Not filled with demonic forces of hatred.

My love for you is wider than any ocean and deeper than any sea,
Allow me to come into your precious heart and I'll prove it to thee.

JESUS

CHARM

WHEN YOUR BACK IS AGAINST

WHEN YOUR BACK IS AGAINST THE WALL

Sometimes life seems as though our back is always against the wall. It is God's way of strengthening us in areas where we are weak, to be honest with you. All of us need to learn about endurance (withstand-hardship-suffering). <u>Christ learned obedience through what he suffered, Hebrews 5:8.</u> In addition, this builds up our character to handle things and everyday life trials and tribulations with confidence (faith). God has previously given us assurance that he has taken over the problem. It is up to us to trust in him to be honest with you. We need to concentrate on the Holy One who can handle what we cannot. He is holding that thing in the palm of his hand.

Remember in the book of Job, how God had confidence in Job knowing that he was not going to let him down. God would like all of us to get to that point. We let God down all the time. Look at how things started happening to Job. He lost everything in a short period. He lost family members, material things that may have had sentimental value to him. God allowed Satan to go forth with attacks on Job property, children and on his health.

You need to watch your so-called friends. <u>Here is a prime example of how</u> people look at the way Christians live or their lifestyle. They are waiting on something to go wrong or for you to make a mistake, <u>so that they can make their assumption.</u> His friends assumed that his suffering came to him this way because he had wronged God. That he had done something, which was not pleasing to God's sight.

Whether you come to the knowledge of what is going on or not, this is Job's test. Everybody has one, his test is to see how he believes in God, trust in God, fear God, and love God. He refuses to give the devil any glory. You know when you give that stupid devil any thing he's going to take that thing and run. Job was an upright man. **He came upon some unpleasant situations, but with his faith, God's strength, he patiently waited (Job 42).** He humbled himself before God and was satisfied. He also waited the devil out. God blessed him twofold of everything he lost. His back was against the wall.

Genesis 22

Abraham was a man of God also, placed in a difficult position. Let me enlighten you a little about Abraham and Sarah waiting on God to move in their life. They had been asking God to bless them with a son. They tarried for many years. So here comes God showing up in his own time, not ours. He blessed them with a son named Isaac.

He too had his back against the wall. God asked him to take his only son to the mountain and offer him as a burnt offering (kill him). Now he has waited all these years to receive this son. Look at how God wanted to test him. Then again, we still have to trust God for who he is. Just to let you know he truly believed in God. He has specific instructions on what to do.

Genesis 22:5 Let's look at it closer than normal. Abraham asked the young men to stay; <u>**we**</u> will come back to you. He already believed in God for the sacrifice. Although it had not happened yet, Abraham used the word <u>**we**</u> by faith, <u>"we will come back to you."</u> As if he knew the God he served was going to do something, he just did not know what. Then to remember he also had a relationship with God. Obviously, he had enough **faith** to know God did not give him a son just for him to kill. Genesis 22:7 Isaac questioned his father, where is the offing? Abraham answered, God himself will provide. His servant was in position to slain his son, God stopped Abraham. He looked up; **God showed up and showed out, there was a ram in the bush.** You may have heard the saying, <u>he may not come when we want him, but he is always on time.</u>

I would think after this day Abraham and God relationship went to another level. He trusts God and God trust him knowing he feared him in a respectable way. This is the place where all of us need to be. Just out of obedience, God blessed all of Abraham's off springs. Abraham knew whom to call on, Jehovah Jireh, the Provider.

Therefore, when your back is against the wall with issues of life, be mindful of Job and how he waited. Abraham also waited on and obeyed God. Each time Jehovah Jireh showed up.

In Jesus Precious Name

CHARM

WHEN YOUR BACK IS AGAINST THE WALL

God allows the just to be put to the test,
Not only by him, but also sometimes by the pest.

You may think you have it all together,
God may have to take it to bless you better.

We the people have to remain steadfast,
Acknowledge God, believing trouble doesn't always last.

Decease, sickness, trials may fall upon your life for a season,
For what the eyes can see no apparent reason.

You may not say you regret, doubt or confusion has arise,
But, we are only human; our faith seems to be down-size.

Go down on your knees, and call upon thee,
Not only to open doors, that is also the key.

So when your back is against the wall,
Believe, have faith, pray and trust before you make the **call.**

In Jesus Precious Name

Amen,

CHARM

Part II

STORIES WITHOUT POEMS

ARE YOU A SLAVE?

If someone was to ask me that question, point blank without thinking the answer would be, **No and don't intend on being one any time soon.** Then if they would have asked me the question at one point in my life according to how I felt on that particular day, I would have to ask them a question <u>"what era are you living in?" (With an attitude).</u>

Slave–person owned by another person; enslave by a habit.
Servant - one who is employed by another for domestic duties.
Prisoner-person deprived of liberty, confinement, kept under involuntary restraint.

Paul says he is a prisoner of (Lord) Jesus in Philemon 1:1. That should be enough to make you think hmm. Now Paul was a man inspired by God, then I must be a slave of Jesus also. If I am not slaving for Jesus Christ, who or what am I serving, Jesus said, "Follow Me." Prisoners are normally restrained to do serious (hard) time. This is the way I understand Paul. He was captive physically, but was a prisoner of Jesus, he belonged to Christ, body, mind and Soul.

Slaves or servants usually have a master. A master usually has a Kingdom, which he rules. Paul loves his master and has every intention on doing serious work for God. Paul's cause was because of Jesus, who is better to be captive for? Keep in mind to him <u>***it is all about Jesus.***</u> When you gave your life to Christ as a Christian, you now belong to him, his property. You can't just give him a piece of you. He should have everything of what you are made of. A mind, staying on him, a heart of compassion, **soul to soul, his connecting to yours,** and a free spirit without bondage of any kind. Or is it that you just went through the verbal motions to accept him to please someone on earth and did not mean a word you said.

Paul also gave me the impression that he was a servant of Jesus. Not only was he called but also he accepted the conversion as the beginning of a new life. After his ordeal on the road to Damascus were very real to him when he took on his new position. Yes he was a novice (amateur) but serious about the Lord's work that needed to go forth. He was chosen to work diligently for God. Slaves or servants do as their Master tells them. They do not mumble or grumble; the majority of them are obedient. Most servants just answer with the response "Yes Lord." Will there be anything else Master that I can do for you? How often do we ask the Lord that question? Then when he tells us, some of us rebel because when the question was asked, you did not mean it from your heart. As time passes you may have forgotten, and find yourself asking God for something again.

God called Paul specifically to get a job done, just as we were called to work the field, bringing in the crop from the harvest. Some of us work harder on a job for man than we would ever attempt to do for God. We look at those jobs as if they are our resource (support) leaning on man. The job that man has given to you does not promise any tomorrows. The security (resource) you get for slaving for the will of God gets you eternal life, which is well worth it. Paul was a man of determination, when it came to the Trinity (God, Jesus, and Holy Spirit) his job was without limitations. He had the attitude **"<u>by any means necessary</u>," and <u>at all cost</u>.**

If you are a servant or God or enslaved for God, be mindful at one point in our lives the element spirits (cigarettes, drugs, alcohol, etc.) of the world enslaved us. Some had terrible habits that you did not want to break, had you under control. All of these habits were spirits that had become habitual and controlling. They were only used to destroy the temple of God and corrupt the mind. The divers of spirits will have the mind so defiled until it will have you believing that you can't do without it. **Satan had us entangled to him as "a slave of sin."**

<u>Thank God, there is another side.</u> When we look at it from the other side, it is a lot better. **Jesus has become habit forming in me, inside out for a while now**; all the Glory belongs to God. I just can not do anything without him. I need him in my life every second of the day. Jesus, having him in our lives has become a constant habit that should enslave us all daily. Instead of being hooked on different spirits of the world, <u>get hooked on Jesus.</u>

According to the promise in the book of Galatians 4:1-6, if we are in Christ, you are a seed of Abraham, you are an heir of Christ, <u>if you belong to Christ.</u> After we have called on **Abba Fathe**r which is an intimate relationship with God, like Jesus has with God. The cry that Jesus called out was Abba Father **(meaning Daddy)** in today's time. We are no longer a servant, but a son, if you are a son, then you are an heir of God through Christ. I want you to understand that we have taken on the **spirit of adoption**. God's people are not step children. <u>Whatever God has released to Jesus Christ is also released to us, not tomorrow, but right now while we are on earth. The miracle is in </u>your mouth.

So if you were to come to me now and allow me to answer the question again. Before I had a lack of knowledge of what a slave truly was. Now since I have been enlightened to looking at things from a spiritual aspect. **I probably have to answer "yes I am a slave".**

I am a **F**ree slave in the spirits of the Lord, I believe in the move of God.
I am a **R**ich slave; I am the joint heir to Jesus Christ.
I am **E**nslaved, he has become a habit, and I can not do anything without him. I am an **E**ncouraged slave, from the word of God.

I am owned by a <u>Master</u> who owns a <u>Kingdom </u>and who has <u>All Power on Heaven and on Earth</u>. He is the King of Kings. He is the Lord of Lords.

Jesus Christ Is My Lord

CHARM

BENEFITS

I do not know why but some people think it's all about them. All the things we do, our actions or the way we response to a circumstance, things we say should not be just to benefit us. It is supposed to benefit the glorification of the Lord Jesus Christ our savior.

The truth of the matter is, while we are placing an application for employment, questions always arise. What are the benefits? How is the pay? Do they have health insurance, or vision care? Well you know I need a job with good benefits. You benefit if you don't know it; it is in your job when you work for God. More than any natural jobs can ever give you. Accept God's benefits package. You will receive health, vision, and excellent raises.

Health Package consists of healing after healing. I sure there are a number of healings that you are not aware of. Healing gives you an opportunity to live and not die. His strips heal us.

Vision Package will have you seeing things you could never see with natural eyes. See when god gives vision, he gives vision. With God's spirit, you get Wisdom, Understanding & Spiritual Knowledge. No matter how large the corporation you are working at, that is one of the best vision packages you are going to get.

The Raises God himself takes you to levels that no man can ever take you. He has treasures, gifts, and bonuses just because he loves the work that you are doing for him. He really appreciates you and is not ashamed to bless you abundantly; he has also fixed it so that you can come live in the penthouse with him. Now that's a plus!

Christ has given us a benefit package that no man could ever match. He has healed our bodies so that we are able to work for him always. He has given us vision to see what he wants us to see –spiritual things. Our minds are to think beautiful thoughts of him.

Joy in our hearts to have laughter.

Peaceable spirit while we go through we can still have joy.

Peace & Joy works together you know, just like Faith & Hope. To get a little deep with it, let's say, just like Jesus & Christ. You cannot have one without the other. Amen.

The extra bonus that we will get is to have life eternal with him.

If you live for God now, you can live with him forever.
Furthermore, if you live for Satan now, you can perish with him eternal.

Whom do you want to work for God or Satan?
Which benefit package is for you?

JESUS

CHARM

MARCH 8, 1999

Dear Christians,

Something happened today that I never experienced before. The Holy Spirit was **angry.** As I was praying the Holy Spirit started speaking through me. He was very upset. He spoke about Christians, how we do not witness the way we should. That all that claims to be Christians and do not want to labor or witness to lost souls. Too many lost souls are still out there, to say everyone wants to claim to be a Christian. We are sitting in the pews to get a word from the Pastors. Some are waiting on the other Christian to work and get the job is done. Every Christian should be working in their area. He is tired of calling on us and we are not there for him, then yet we call upon him in the middle of the night. He is there, but he wakes us up in the night to pray, we are too tired to hear what he has to say. Nevertheless, he still blesses us.

We are always coming to GOD asking for blessings. When Holy Ghost comes to us, we put him off until later. He has been available for us but we are not available for him. He said he is soon to come. The Christians need to work hard to bring in the crop. He is not sending his son back again. He left us power and authority and we are to work for him. We are not giving him 90% of our time. He says we are lazy and slothful Christians. If he was to come now, his Christians are not ready, some who think they will make it to heaven will not. A lot of work still needs to be done, I am soon to come. I am soon to come, and a lot of my work has not been completed.

He also spoke about babes in Christ, he is expecting the to work hard at what they know, He says he will do the talking, just go out to minister.

I have never heard that tone of voice with the Holy Spirit before. He is grieving for us, because we are not ready. **We need to get busy for the Lord.**

Thank God for God

JESUS
CHARM

GO PASS TO EXCEL

Definition Webster: Pass- go pass; leave behind; go across, over; meet requirements of: Act of passing: success in a test or gap-road.

Surpass- Excel, go beyond- transcend (go beyond limits of).

As I gather my thoughts together I would like to share them with you. In order to excel-transcend or go beyond. You need to do one step before going to the next level. We as the people have to go to Pass. Meaning you go through the fire, swim out from the bank of the river and go into the deep.

To be successful in our everyday lives, we can't settle for just passing the test. But, still yet there are tests we have to pass or we will see them again. As we take our journey with Christ, let's go beyond the limits. Not just in material pleasures, but in spiritual pleasure as well. Seek out wisdom, knowledge, understanding and illumination in the world of God. Once you have acknowledged your purpose, that will definitely help you (us) go pass to Excel. I believe the word of God will bring you closer to him, illuminating you with hope until your faith gets built up to his most holy faith. Before you know it, you are ready to go to the limits.

1. Excelling your mind on the word of God.
2. Excelling your heart on the spirit of God, connecting without any confusion or doubt.
3. Excelling your soul unto God.

The mere thought of passing and straight to Excel is more than enough to give God the glory. Just think each time you pass something whether in a car, boat, or achieving a goal, you are expecting to see something before you. Paul said in <u>Philippians 3:14, press forward toward the mark for the prize of the high calling of God in Jesus Christ.</u> In other words we have been set up to run the Christian race. Your goal is to win the prize in heaven, regardless of what is behind us. Keep focus on what is before you which is heaven. In order for this to work out for your good, we have to go pass, pass to leave behind and cross over to meet the requirement to have the success you need to surpass, and transcend to get beyond the limits.

I believe that once you get to a certain point of passing the test that Jesus has in stored for you, **not a devil in hell can stop you**. By his might and your obedience you can conquer anything your heart desires according to his will. Our goal should be like Jesus **"The Goal of Beyond the Limits". Excel!**

In Jesus Precious Name

CHARM

HE SPARED US

There are so many ways to die - natural causes, fire, shootings, stalking, sickly decease, a simple operation in the hospital, car accidents, airplane crash, innocent lump on the head, choking to death. Many more ways that can take our lives. God has chosen to spare us. He has life in the palm of his hand, just like everything else. God is in control of life and death.

People don't die because of these instances. God had to make that choice. You can choose eternal life or death. <u>Death in sin or alive in Christ</u>. You shall live and not die. He decided to allow you to wake up this morning sure as you are reading this message.

Take a moment and think how many times God has spared your life from some of these occurrences. He spared your life hoping that you would appreciate it. He spared your life on this earth – so you can have life more abundantly. He spared your life so that you can assist in giving life to someone who is not as wise as you or not as fortunate as you. This is so you can encourage someone – inspire someone to open his or her spiritual eyes to see <u>God's salvation</u> plan.

God has spared you long enough to read this message and make an intelligent decision, **now you can choose life over death or death over life. The choice is yours.**

He spared us …again.

Bless his Holy Name.

CHARM

I MESSED AROUND AND FELL IN LOVE

You know how you are introduced to someone, well it happened to me. I met him years ago, I wasn't looking, and did not care about much at the time. To tell you the truth sometimes you just don't want to be bothered with anyone, not even with yourself. I know no one else feels like that but me, **(Yeah right)**. Therefore, in doing what comes natural to me, I brushed him off every time someone came to introduce him. I would say anything just to get him to leave me alone.

He was too serious for me, at a young age. I felt I was too young for a relationship with anyone. The truth of the matter is he did not stop coming, but he did let me know he would be there for me. At that particular time, I was in my own little world. Being honest, I just didn't care much about what he had to say.

I realized that time was getting away from me. I was getting older and time waited for no one. I Was ready to settle down and get married. Well then, I was keeping my eyes open wide for the one that was so interested in me. Not knowing he was still waiting on me. That was so nice of him, but I realize that he was born with that compassionate heart. I was so happy, had me bubbling with joy.

I thanked God for allowing him to wait on me. God truly blessed me with one of the most precious gifts in my life. When I finished acting foolish and gave into him, I cannot complain.

He has shared his love that he longed to give me for so many years. I never knew someone could love me like that. I no longer have an empty void in my life. When that kind of love is being expressed and shared in that way, you cannot do nothing but return it. I could have continued being unappreciative, but I needed to change my ugly ways. He is always there for me even when I think that I can handle the situation, he shows up. He's constantly assisting, giving me gifts and loving me unconditionally. I am going to let you know I have never met any one like him in my lifetime, he is the only one for me. I do want you to know I decided not to let this one got away. I want to give him all of me for the rest of my days on this earth.

From day one, he has been better to me than I have been to myself. Words can not explain his love. His actions cannot be expressed. Now I am happily married to him and well pleased with our relationship. I have to tell you **" I messed around and fell in love."** I thank God that the feelings are mutual, **because you first loved me**. *I forgot to introduce you to my* husband, this is my beloved Jesus.

I love you Lord Jesus

CHARM

IT'S JUST A LOAN

My house is not my house.

Yes, I live there, I take residence there, I even take care of it, Jesus abides there also. I'm just like a hitchhiker, passing through this world. Expecting my home is in the Kingdom of God eternally. By not accepting Jesus as our Lord and Saviour while passing through, obviously you have already accepted Hell as your home eternally. God has given it to me for a season, "It's Just a Loan".

EWO is not my church.

This is a building where I attend to Praise and Worship the Living God.

Many people attend church religiously. They are in the church, but is the church in them? Knowing Jesus personally, Learning the word of God and your body is your church, where the temple of the Holy Ghost resides. This is a building, "It's Just a Loan."

My eyes are not my eyes.

These two eye sockets, they are not mine. I do thank God for being able to see physical (tangible) things. Also these things that we see are temporal (2 Cor 4:18). They too will pass away, but the word of God shall stand forever (Isaiah 40:8). To get full clarification is like seeing the unseen or seeing if you understand something. Let's just say "seeing with your spiritual eyes". Looking at things in a different perspective, with wisdom, knowledge and with understanding, "It's Just a Loan".

When you (I) use the word my, it takes on possession. My car, my church, my home, etc… When we can get very personal about something and get an attitude if someone makes a comment about **our stuff.**

Get personal with Jesus as you do with your stuff. He will bless you beyond measure. This stuff is not yours, all of it belongs to GOD.((KJV) John 1:1-3, In the beginning was the word, the word was with God, and the word was God. The same was in the beginning with God. All things was made by him; and without him was not anything made that was made. Genesis 1:1 says in the beginning God created heaven and the earth. He was already here, now where were you with your stuff?

We need to claim Jesus like we claim that stuff we say is ours. He is just merely giving us a loan for a season. Even though we paid for it in the earthly realm. When we leave this world, the same way we came in, **without nothing.**

Spiritually you should Thank God that he has allowed you to material things. Deuteronomy 8 speaks about not forgetting God in prosperity. He made it all. In all that you give, give thanks to God. Remember God giveth and God taketh away.

It's Just A Loan

JESUS

CHARM

OPEN HOUSE

Open house allows you to take your time and look around. Observe the good qualities of the house that is well pleasing to you. Plenty of houses have bad qualities too. Of course, everything has a place, and it will be in its place. You have been invited; take your time to pursue. Peep at every inch as close as you can. Go into the closets, in every room, bathrooms, yards, and walk on the land, soft spots, and check out the roof; you will be able to ask questions. *Hoping you will get the truth,* taking notes, trying to remember to ask questions as they arise, in addition with everything this person is telling you about the house. They are trying to sell it, and obviously, you are trying to buy it.

The big day has arrived to sign the papers for one of the most important investments you may ever have to sign. It is as an open house when you were getting ready to purchase it. Now that all the papers are in tack, it is the closing of the house. You have to sign plenty of papers for the Closing of the house. Here is where the assumption takes place: this is my house. You're wrong, nothing really belongs to us, God Blesses us, but we are borrowing from Christ. You are still borrowing this house just like the rest of us. Christ just loans it to you for a season.

Any time you are not sure of a new circumstance then you ask questions, just as you would do for the new house. You ask all kinds of questions until you get clarification or you are at peace with the answers that the realtor is giving you. Ask God anything you want he will give the correct answer that is according to his will. Sometimes it may not be what we want to hear. It really does not matter what his answer is; he is still God. While you were checking out that house, there was a closet door and you opened it, to see how large of space the closet have, you did not knock before you opened it, you just did it. Christ knocked at your heart's door and is waiting on you to say, "please come in." Outside the door, there is a respectable, gentle spirit waiting, he is not coming in unless he's invited. He is a gentleman with good hospitality. He will give you anything your heart desires in his will, as you commit yourself to him, then he shall bring it to pass. (Psalms 37:4-5) He will treat you the way you love to be treated. The bible says

<u>A</u>sk <u>S</u>eek <u>K</u>nock and ask again. The door shall be open. Heart and arms are open to you; <u>he's available, are you?</u>

That is awesome how you are seeking a house and <u>he is seeking your soul</u> to come and live in your house. Wanting so much to finish what he has started in your life, by turning your life over to him. If you don't belong to God then you belong to Satan. Your body is the temple of the Holy Ghost. Jesus wants to live in you.

He is always blessing you, giving you chance after chance, day after day to just invite him in. Who do you think you are hurting, by not accepting his gift? **The things that you are searching for in your life, he has it.** Sounds like to me, you need him. If you have not accepted him, then you have rejected him. John 1:8-13 " world knew him not, went to his own and they received him not." When you do not accept him as your Lord and Savior, Matthew 7:23 speaks of him not being able to recognize you at heaven's door and will also say depart from me I know you not. I do not believe anyone wants the Lord to turn him or her away. So why are you turning him away when he is knocking at your door? Are you moving into this new house that he decided to give you? Therefore, you are going to leave him outside knocking. That is very rude of you to treat him like that. Psalms 100 says," Enter into my gates with thanksgiving and into my courts with praises," be thankful. God has given you uncountable blessings; at this time bless his Holy Name.

You are trying to make sure everything is in order before you close on this new house. Well Jesus wants to purge you, get you ready to move everything that does not belong out of the way. He has opened the door for you to enter this new home. He may decide to let you go through a season of preparation. Getting you prepared to come in and serve him. The Holy Spirit is in control of everything. Are you aware that Christ has given you an open proposal to come into his house repeatedly? Open arms to meet you at the door every time you call on his name, he is there. You are seeking good substructure (foundation) for your house. Read Matthew 7:24-27. Will it be able to stand through rain, hail, hurricanes, tornadoes etc? Christ my friend is your foundation on solid ground.

Moreover, he has enlightenment of the storms that you will go through. That accepting him you **shall** win the victory.

When you are born this is called a **physical birth.** The second time you are born this is a **spiritual birth by accepting, believing and confessing Christ as your Lord and Savior,Romans 10:9-13.** If you have not received a degree from the Holy One, the others that you may have are temporary, they will pass away, but the B.A.C.D. **(Born Again Christian Degree) will stand as long as you permit it.**

Jesus Christ has given you an open invitation for **your Open House** (your body), that is the temple of the Holy Ghost through his beautiful eyes. According to The Bible this spiritual house, everything must be in order. Open your house to Jesus today.

Most of the time, we are expecting our blessings to fall in place, in order and on time.

God expects us to fall in place with his commandments, in order to his will, and on time with obedience.

CHARM

JESUS

READY OR NOT HERE I COME

When we were young, you and I both played all types of games. We played tag, hiding, go seek, jump rope, football just to name a few. The game playing days is now over. It's time to grow up and become who God has called us to be. Sometime we may tell or mention to someone that "we are grown and no one is going to disrespect us, talk to us or treat us like we are children. Well to tell you the truth, we are still childish in some areas of our lives.

Some of you say you are grown but still playing some type of game. The bible says in I Corinthian 13:11 "When I was a child, I spoke as a child; but when I became a man (woman) I put away childish things". Stick around a person long enough, you'll see how the real person will come out - especially if they can't have their way with something. The reaction of grown folks, pouting, mumbling saying things that they wouldn't normally say if they were to have it their way. Women love to cry to have things in their court. Whether you know it, that's a form of manipulation. Just like a child – when they want attention. Men mostly just get quiet. Trying to hide that little boy's crushed feelings. All of that and more, you know the things you do, I don't have to call all of them out. That's just merely the little boy or girl being exposed "so much to say for them adults".

What about the grown folks who's not speaking to someone because "they say she don't like me". Question: Did that person ever say it to you? Another one we all have heard -- - She doesn't speak to me so I don't speak to her. Have you ever thought you can speak first, just as well as the other person? The childish games people play. God love a peacemaker (Matt 5:9). Maybe you need to stop playing games, humble yourself, allow him to change you from those wicked ways. If you do or if you don't "ready or not he's coming."

You know when it gets down to the God honest truth, we all want to be treated as an adult and acting like a child. Even after a child has an argument with another child or upset with someone, they talk, play, forgive and forget. As adults you should know better, this foolishness will hinder your blessings. We need all the blessings we can get. Let Go and Let God. If acting like this, you've got to be a babe in Christ. Who cares (or so what) if you've been in the church for years. You are not growing with Christ with that nasty attitude. Most likely only because you have not allowed the fullness of God to reign in your life to the point of being in total control. Then again, we are so grown. You are not but so grown without him teaching you his ways.

Some of our minds have not fully developed enough to trust him in all things. Bless his Holy Name; give him back just a portion of what he has invested in you. **Believe in the manifestation of how he conquered life, death and the grave.** The awesome power of his resurrection. Trust that in or out of season he's there. Knowing that your heart, mind soul and spirit can handle the confession from your lips. God knows your heart and the belief of God. Believe also that Jesus is the Son of the Living God and the power of the Holy Spirit. Ready or not he's coming back seeking hearts without a spot or wrinkle.

This should help you get a fresh start being able to handle *"Ready or Not Here I Come."* He is coming back whether we like it or whether we are ready for him. We have no choice in the matter, **but we do have choices**. Every creature that God created, every soul on the face of this earth, (Rms: 4:11)every tongue will confess and every knee shall bow. Let everything that has breath, praise the Lord. Exodus 20:3 say; Shall not put no other gods before me. **All will have to choose what God they will serve.**

If you decide you are not ready to serve God, that is your choice. If you decide you need to get yourself together before you come to him, that is your choice. Even if you decide this is not a good time in your life, because you have too much chaos going on, that too is your choice. Maybe that's why you have chaos because you have not made the correct choice to your life the *"main ingredient" in your daily activity.* Let's say you don't have time for God right now. God has all the **time** in the world, **time** belongs to him, the question is do you? He doesn't move according to a clock. But he is so gracious he manage his busy day to wake you up long enough to read this. Do not let time fool you. Time is short and can be cut shorter at any given time. Maybe in the back of your mind you will get ready for him later. <u>Even though tomorrow is not promised to anyone.</u> "When you make that choice-then you take that chance". Whatever your excuse or reason you may think of to tell someone - - - "It's OK" because that is your choice. ***"Ready or Not Here I Come."***

The Bible says he will not make any introduction speeches. **Rev. 3:3** – <u>remember</u> therefore how thou hast received and heard, and hold steadfast and repent. If therefore thou shalt not watch, I will come on thee as a thief and thou shalt not know what hour I <u>will come upon thee.</u> The way I see it is, we heard the gospel, we received the truths in which we heard and we have repent when we changed our views or feelings toward the gospel. We don't have to watch because we have been warned that he will come suddenly, unannounced. You won't have time to repent once he comes. Thieves don't let you know they are going to break in. Some folks are ready to surprise a thief some are not. You have to be prepared, be expecting him at any given time. Live your life everyday, as it was your last. Jesus was speaking in Matthew 24:35-36. Heaven and earth shall pass away, but my words shall not pass away. **Verse 36** says but of that day and hour knoweth no man, not the angels in heaven, **<u>but my father only. So don't try to figure it out, by calling that 800# on TV – reading tabloids. No one knows but God himself.</u>**

Just to bring something back to your memory, one day in Greensboro, NC snow fell a a few years ago while everyone on day shift was at work. It was definitely chaos – no one could get anyone on the phone – lines were tied up, traffic backed up, power outages, grocery stores packed, people buying up everything they could think of. A twenty minute drive home took about 1-½ hours to 2 hours. City was at a stand still. This storm was not announced, but it took everyone by surprise. **"Ready or Not, Here I Come."**

Similar situation happened unannounced in the forecast at 9:30 am. Winds came from nowhere 20 to 30 mph, tore the city up. There were power outages, trees down, accidents, thousands of dollars in damage. No one knew. **"Ready or Not Here I Come."**

God has done everything he know to do, he sent prophets, left us with a manual to guide us, allowed his son to shed blood for our sins. Then he gives us Grace and Mercy daily with his blessings. **This is an awesome God.** He played as fair as a game can be played. When the game is over – **everyone will know the sound of the trumpet.** "Ready or Not Here I Come."

Have Mercy on us

Lord In Jesus Name

CHARM

REAL VS REALITY

R=REAL

E=EXPERIENCES

A=ASSEMBLED

L=LOGIC

In other words, Genuine Knowledge and Wisdom are together fitting with a convincing force.

Real in the world people want to see for themselves if it is real. Truth of the matter, they do not believe what they see sometimes with their own eyes. You may hear them say, I will believe it when I see it for myself. Nevertheless, when it truly happens they have a problem with it, start-asking questions, and "can it really be"?

The word real really means: genuine, and not artificial.

Do you believe the acts of God, if not then you do not believe in God, he is Real as it gets? How can you believe in God and do not accept him nor the recognition of his authority over everything that you set your eyes on, belongs to God Almighty. That's something how we, the people, can watch the news and believe everything they see just because it was on TV on the internet. When each and everyday we open our eyes to God manifesting himself to us personally, letting us not only see his realness but also living in his realness. Hopefully the day will come when you can realize just how concrete the existence of this is an awesome God that we are not real with, is so genuine to us.

Come to think of it, let's examine real money and play money. The difference is that play money does not have any value, it is not worth anything, and it is just that, play. Real Money has value, worth something according to how much money you have. It's important because worthiness makes it important. For some reason or another I don't know

why or understand some folks that don't have a relationship with God, never been introduced to him, or have had an encounter with the Holy

Spirit but **bold enough to say they do not believe in him.** However, people accept that Satan is real. Now where do you think that demonic sad creature came from. Somebody had to create him. God is worthy of every thing that your life consists of today. Now you can make the decision and accept that he is real. Then again, you can be ignorant and believe that you are doing all this yourself. Worship him this day in spirit and in truth. There will come a day, you will seek to find out if he is the real thing and will not be able to find him. God is not worthy just for what he can do, better yet, just because of who he is, and for what he has already done, for you and I, which is more than enough.

Now when you finish making a complete fool out of yourself, allow realism to set in and take over. Once that happens you need to read a doctrine that the universe exists outside the mind, which is the living word of God **(The Bible)**. It is your manual for your life or **B**iblical **I**nstructions **B**efore **L**eaving **E**arth. All of mankind needs to know about the Father, the Son and the Holy Spirit. Ask for God's forgiveness; ask that he may have mercy upon you (Romans 10:9-11). Please we, do not want to forget (Romans 12:2)renewing of the mind, that you have a new way of thinking.

Speaking of reality, Jesus came to earth in the flesh. Personally speaking, that was a fact and consists of a real event that amounts to Reality. **Reality amounts to a real event and consist of as a fact**. Now some people still have a problem believing that God and Jesus is the same, still yet one. Our logic would never be equivalent to the Creator of this world. Fearing the Lord is the beginning of Wisdom, fear (reverent) in this sense meaning to Respecting him (Proverbs 9:10). Another thing you will need is Faith, to see the manifestation of his blessings and knowledge of the Holy One's understanding. Faith is the substance of things hope for, evidence of things not seen(Hebrews 11:1). You are just hoping for something that you do not have, but you just know by faith, it is on the way. If you do not believe, you are lacking in faith.

Then again they have some people claim to be Christians and afraid of Satan. That reminds me of a double-minded man being unstable in all his ways (James 1:8). **Jesus** says in the book of Matthew 10:28, "fear not them that which kill the body, but not able to kill the soul: but rather fear him who is able to destroy both soul and body in hell." I hope that you make the right decision and try God. <u>Just ignore Satan, he does not care about you or your soul burning in hell eternally.</u> That is where he is and where he is going to stay. That pitiful creature can't repent and get out but God has given you another opportunity to come in from under that demonic curse of the adversary.

The <u>adversary</u> takes a real life situation, <u>puts it into action</u>. First, you think of it, then you think about it just a little bit too long, now it is hanging out on your mind all the time. Next thing you know Satan has dramatized it, have your mind going from one step of drama to another. Now you are trying to figure out how you are going to handle this circumstance and come out on top. Well I do not want to bust your bubble, but if you know to call upon the name of the Lord, now is a very good time. Because you need his help, without him you can't do anything. That thing called a stronghold has totally overtaken your mind. If only you would have known to cast down on every thought and imagination that exalts against the word of God. <u>You would not have had your brain bombarded with that mess.</u>

For example, when you see a magic trick, they say eyes don't lie, but still you can see some strange stuff happens with magic tricks. The devil plays tricks on your eyes and mind to make you think this is really happening. You and I know no one can float in air that has to be an illusion (deception). Just like Satan, a deceiving spirit. Jesus walked on water that was a miracle (supernatural) powers (Matthew 14:25). Jesus and all his works that he did were real and at rest at this hour.

Fairy tales is another form of deception that man will believe a lie over the truth just because. All that stuff is making people believe it is the truth. People love illusions, deception, and make believe. All that is unnecessary foolishness rattling your brain and invading your thoughts. When you get ready to compare real and reality remember this; real is as genuine as reality is to fact.

Reality is in the word of God, he will teach you everything you need to know about his character. Trust him with all things. Allow him to be the light under your feet to guide you into **the Kingdom**, where you can live with him forever, **in Jesus Name.**

CHARM

SOMEONE CALLED ME

So many times, we have been alone at home or maybe at work and have asked the question "Who called my name?" If you were to answer and say "What" do not be surprised by the next voice you hear or where it is coming from. Most of the time, there is always somebody standing right behind you with a certain look asking whom are you talking to, no one did not call you. You may say something like, excuse me I thought I heard someone call me. If you are anything like me, you play that thing off with a joke. Knowing you heard your name loud and clear.

This brings me to the Old Testament I Samuel Chapter 3. To make a long story short, Samuel was a young boy. The Lord was ministering to him under the Priest Eli. When he went to lie down to go to sleep. The Lord called Samuel, Samuel answered, "Here am I " but he went to Eli. He told him I did not call you. Samuel did this three times. The third time Eli told Samuel the next time he calls you to answer by saying **"Speak Lord your servant is listening."**

When the Lord calls his children, he will call you by name. Exodus 3:17, the Lord spoke to Moses and said *"I know thee by name."* He created us, so he knows us very well. Before we have spoken the words out of our mouth, God is aware of what we were going to say. Just make sure you know his voice. The Bible says, "My sheep know my voice**." John 10:27 says: "My sheep hear my voice and I know them.**

God knows you and you should know him. That means you and God should have a lot of conversations together. Next time your Father calls you, just answer by saying, **"Speak Lord your servant is listening"**.

That will please him to know you hearken to his voice. The next thing is being obedient to the voice of the Lord.

JESUS

CHARM

S-S-S-S

You can just about choose any alphabet to get someone's attention, but you have to keep their attention which is vital also. I decide to use the 4's, maybe because it reminds me of the word "start". God started at the beginning with the word. John 1:1 said in The <u>beginning was the word and the word was with God</u>, the word was God. John 1:14 said 'The word was made flesh and dwelt among us.' Jesus is the true living word in the flesh.

Savior- one who saves.

That flesh was the first (s), which is the **Savior** of the World. Savior is a person that saves, like Jesus Christ. Isaiah 43:11 reveals to us that beside me (Jesus) there is no savior. So if you are expecting some other God (astrologers –palm reader, etc.) to do or tell you some miraculous things, keep on living, it just wants to happen in this lifetime. Jesus is the one and only one that you can believe in and receive eternal life. If you do not know him then you can not believe in him, get acquainted with him on a personal level. Romans 10:9 will assist you to become the saint that God would have you be that he may be glorified. When you die with him, spiritually just begin to live.

Saint-holy person, unselfish-patient.

Becoming a **Saint** is really a new position, just like holding on to a job. You have to then start at the beginning and be taught how to be raised up to sainthood (canonize). Jesus will help you if you are ***willing*** to be helped, every step of the way. You have to have zealous spirit along with a teachable spirit as well. You have to understand some people are not willing to unlearn the wrong (old) way to be taught the correct way. This is why it is vital to be willing, and you already have the best teacher to do the teaching for you, your Big Brother Jesus. The Big Brother will teach you everything you need to know to live on this earth. He will not mistreat you, lead you astray, or deceive you. He will give you the very best at being perfect. As he brings you up on top of things as they arise, Jesus can also rise you above the circumstance (s) in his world. It is like a promotion, see now you have power and authority to trample on the devil's head. Luke 10:19-20 says nothing shall by any means hurt you. Rejoice, because your names are written in heaven. You cannot do this thing alone; you need the Savior to survive.

Survivor- (noun) keeps existing-outlast.

Every morning we awake to another day not knowing the things God were doing while we were asleep. We may feel that we made it, but you have to realize that you have to still Survive through the rest of the day, still yet another night, not knowing if you truly survive the test of God. This world can be rough for even the toughest sinner. The want- to-be's need to have some knowledge of how to survive in the business world, as well as the streets. Whether you are in church or out you need the Savior to Survive out here. Every one of us, everyday receives new Grace and Mercy. Without the twins, we could not survive in this world. If you are a saint or sinner, you need to know what it take to survive. It is the power of the Holy One. You have to overcome obstacles, hindrances, wickedness, and demons on the job, at the store, even divers of spirits in your homes. Maybe this is something that you need to be first, by putting Jesus first in your life to survive. <u>As long as he is first, you will not come in last. You can win, after you submit to23 God, I have never seen the righteous forsaken nor his seed begging for bread</u>. You can not lose when you humble yourself to Christ.

Sinner-transgression, misdeed, wickedness.

All of us were born as sinners, until we came into the knowledge of the Trinity (Father, Son, and Holy Spirit). Some choose to have him to become part of our everyday life. Then yet we are not perfect, but we are forgiven of our sins, Thank God. Sinners choose not to live according to the Savior's will. Let's say you do not know Jesus Christ for yourself, then how are you going to become that saint? Living your life according to his statues, knowing your purpose and destiny. There are some things not adding up. You do not believe in Christ and the power of his resurrection and do not want to be introduced to him. Then you do not really know Satan but you believe in him and how well he deceives you. If you truly knew Satan than you would run away from him instead of with him to hell. In case you are just plain ignorant to that fact that you are lining yourself right behind the devil. You can overcome the sins because Jesus has paid the price.

Revelation 3:15-16 says God will not have you lukewarm, neither hot or cold. Think about it that is like being a _Sinful Saint or better yet a Little Pregnant._

Either Jesus Christ saves you or _Satan will save you for himself._

In Jesus Name

CHARM

THE INSTRUCTIONS

God has given each one of us specific instructions of our do's and don't s. There are numerous reasons why we ignore what he has said. We know that the things we do are disobedient, to what the Father has asked of us. Some of our disobedience can be out of ignorance or just stubbornness. Maybe you have no idea of what GOD wants you to do. Perhaps you may feel that you can just be disobedient today and make it up to him later. Thinking just like the world *"shoot first, ask questions later"*.

You may think you can do whatever you want now and repent later? Do you not think that Satan will have you so focused on whatever? He will not allow you to remember to repent later. From that point on, he is laughing at you, knowing that you forgot about repenting to GOD. Something's that have not entered into your mind yet, fleshly things will also have you being disobedient not intentionally, but it will happen. Let us just say you have very good intentions on doing the right thing. <u>GOOD INTENTIONS AND GOOD DEEDS WILL NOT GET YOU INTO HEAVEN.</u> That is not going to work out the way you may think <u>if you believe you can manipulate God</u>. It is necessary that YOU turn away from Sin.

When you are before GOD for judgment, he knows your heart, he knows all about good intentions, however, according to your works and the way you handled the situation. You are going to get judged by God. One thing I do know; "One day all of human mankind will have their day in court". No one will miss this day. GOD will be the JUDGE.

Command: order with authority.   Commandment: precept from God.

The Ten Commandments

Thou shalt have no other Gods before me.

Thou shalt not make or worship other graven image.

Remember the sabbath day, keep it holy.

Thou shalt not take God's name in vain.

Honor thy father and thy mother.

Thou shalt not kill.

Thou shalt not commit adultery.

Thou shalt not steal.

Thou shalt not bear false witness.

Thou shalt not covet.

II Tim 2:15-Study to show thyself approved. Proverbs 8:17-Luke 1:79-Jeremiah 33:3. Seek out the word of GOD for guidance and revelation. He has more commandments and blessings in store for you.

JESUS

CHARM

THE SATAN PRESENTATION

Presentation- Offering; presenting something or someone.
Present-Being there at hand.

To be stated Satan is offering us many things. Such as **SINS** on a silver platter. Making it look so good until our flesh desires to have it. When that occurs he has to be present. He began in the beginning of the Bible in Genesis 3 as a serpent. Temptation has always been one of his favorite games to play with the flesh. The spirit is willing, the flesh is weak. He tempted Adam and Eve the very first time he showed his ugly face.

Then to show you how he doesn't care about you or anything else but making you fall out of the will of God. He approaches the Son of Man boldly with temptation soon after he has fast for forty days and nights. Asking him to turn the stone into bread if thou were the Son of God. If you know Jesus he had a word for him. (Matthew 4.)

He not only comes to you at certain moments, he comes at unsure times as well. The ugly creature will show up at a vulnerable or weak time not because he's looking after you. Vulnerable plotting is putting yourself in the position to be influenced. Just because he feels that's the best time for him to make his attack; hoping he can sneak up on you, and catch you off guard, like cowards do. <u>The devil is a liar and the father of them. John 8:44, also says he was a</u> murderer from the beginning. You can add thief to the list too. John 10:10, speaks of the thief cometh not, but for to steal, kill and destroy.

He not only gets dressed up on Sunday, but he and his imps are always out lurking 24-7. What better place to go on a Sunday other than church? He will be there hiding behind make-up, suits, dresses, you have to understand he perpetrates (something evil, wrong) just like some of us out here in the world, presenting themselves to be some they are not. Acting wise and doing otherwise. Walking around with their heads stuck in the air with their religious attitudes and poisoned minds. Last but not least, and are carrying characteristic traits of the devil. Some are even thinking and believing that Satan's way is the way of the world. <u>Well it is not.</u> Don't be used by the adversary. You mean to tell me it is Ok for the enemy to have his way with you. That is like someone forcing you, or forcing themselves on you to do something that you do not want to do. Well when you give in to the Devil, you have accepted his way.

Satan fixes himself up in disguises, so when it is time to do the presentation it can work like he planned. He also disguises his names as well as circumstances and situations. He will destroy your thought pattern if you are not careful. We have heard a mind is a terrible thing to waste. Why give any thought and imagination that exalts against the word of God to the Devil. (II Corinthians 11:14). He has disguised himself as an angel <u>of light</u>. However, we know he is the Prince of Darkness. Satan will sit in motion with the eyes that are never satisfied. He never has enough, just plain selfish and greedy. Then he wants to attack your mind to start thinking just like that old sly, sneaky scheming serpent. The flesh will start to compromise with the demons that's lurking in the world. <u>*Before you know it, you have made a deal with a demon.*</u> The demon is like an old fool running to let Satan who is the leader and host of evil spirits know that you fell for **"The Satan Presentation."** What about the real one that's fixed up just for you, very well. Just the way you like it, it seems good, giving you feelings that you never had before. Pretending to make a lot of sense at the right time. "Now you have just been bought at an inexpensive price, you were a bargain to him. You have been "<u>Souled Out</u>" to the Devil. Have you ever known the devil to do anything good for someone? He may make you think it is all-good, but get real.

I'm not giving the devil any glory, that is his job is to make us look foolish, some people make his job a little too easy for him. He will try to get you by "**<u>any means necessary</u>**." Spiritual influence is what he uses on God people as often as they allow him. Satan does not have any power, but when someone is always saying Satan is doing this, Satan is doing that, he chest gets all puffed up and thinks he is the man. I have heard some Christians say Satan's name more than Jesus' name. I do not understand. Satan is not in charge of nothing but these little imps. God has all power in his hand. Once you know a person's nature (what they are about) whether it is gossiping, lying, phony, etc. You can choose not to be bothered with them. You take control. Find the nature of the demon, take control and cast him out.

The word evil is live spelled backwards. Satan used to live in heaven until he got the big head. **Lived is devil spelled backwards**. The <u>**evil devil** *shall live in Hell eternal. Now that is the truth.*</u> When you want to do good, evil is always present (Romans 7:21). This is why you need protection, a guard, the Holy Spirit. Do not get caught without it. The devil will surely sift you like wheat. The Holy Spirit is not only a guide, but also a comforter, teacher and keeper of those who want his help. The Holy Spirit will protect your house, which is the temple of the Holy Ghost. Anything that does not belong cannot or will not enter if you have protection. We believe we need protection for everything else in the world. Now tell me why you don't want to receive the protection of the Holy Spirit. Be aware evil spirits are lurking, seeking a place to rest. (Luke 11:23-26) I hope that he will not find a place in your house, In Jesus Name.

Satan is a crazy ugly rascal; you can lock the front door. He will go to the back door, when he doesn't get any response. He will continue standing around trying to figure out what he can do to make you give in to him. When he gets desperate he starts picking the lock, something like finding your weakest spot, or having the children coming home bugged out. He may even try to find something in your past life and bring that thought in your head. I would like you to do something for me, **every time he reminds you of your past, remind him of his future in the lake of fire**. Before you know it, he has entered the door with some inadequate (weak) disguise with a new name. He has made himself up to be in II Corinthians 11:14 as angel of light. The only reason he entered, the door was open, and he did not see a guard of protection. Your spirit of discernment is God speaking, and your discernment did not kick in to work for you. One of the things I know about the Holy Ghost is he does not lie, he would have kept your eyes sharper to pick Satan out, for you to see him coming.

Furthermore, my knowledge of one of his names is Prince of Duplicity (deceit). He only deals with double-dealings, such as two headed coins, fixed dice, etc. You would think deception is his last name. One of his arts is delusion, when he plays with your vision. Still, he has a plausible (convincing) appearance (presentation) to make you believe it is apparently true. This is one of **_Satan's Presentations._**

Satan also has been called the Prince of this World in John 12:31, which will be cast out. Permit me to take you a little further into what Jesus has to say about the devil in Luke 10:17-20. The seventy disciples were asking Jesus is the devil subject to us through thy name (Jesus). Does he have to obey us because he has been cast out? We can command the devil to flee from those who have been possessed. Verse 18 says with Jesus speaking, "I beheld Satan as lightning fell from heaven". He is stating how he noticed Satan how quickly he fell from heaven, as fast it takes lighting to strike. Maybe he also could be saying by the command of the disciples how fast evil spirits would be an outcast. Satan does not have a thing on us, we have him with the authority of Jesus. Verse 19, "Behold I give unto you power to tread on serpents and scorpions, and over all the power of the enemy: and nothing shall by any means hurt you". Jesus will preserve us, his adversaries, his power, and us from the enemy (Satan). Danger can come in for the attack but we are unaffected by any of the wickedness. Satan and his friends can be guarded and covered with nothing less than the Almighty Power of Jesus. Verse 20, "Now withstanding in this rejoice not, that the spirits are subject unto you: but rather rejoice because your names are written in heaven". Although it is a blessing that we have authority over the spirits, but rejoice because we as the people of God are entitled to everlasting life. We are friends of God, and able to dwell with him. **Glory Be to God Almighty.**

We all who know and believe in Jesus Christ that Satan approaching his death will destroy his kingdom. I think he is trying so hard to throw his weight around to put fear in us. Another thing he has claimed for himself as an authority figure. Satan is a great pretender of authority (power or influence). He is definitely not worthy; the poor pitiful little creature has everlasting fire waiting for him. Per Matthew 25:4, "Then shall he say also unto them on the left hand, depart from me,<u>ye cursed, into everlasting fire, prepared for the devil and his angels.</u>" We may not have knowledge of what our future holds, but we do know Satan's.

There has been for a long time conflict between God the Creator of All and the Devil.

However, the victory is already ours. Here are a few things that have gotten my attention I would like to share with you.

Both God and Satan are Spirits they are very real. Both are seeking souls.
Both are knocking at your heart's door.
Both are presenting something (God) Good Gifts and Blessings
God is offering the gift of eternal abundance, life.

<u>**Heaven**</u>

(Satan) unfaithfulness, delusions, lies, doubt, etc.
Satan has nothing to offer but eternal damnation, death.

<u>**Hell**</u>

<u>***If you are going to answer the door, know who it is before you welcome them in.***</u>

I need you to explain something to me, how is it that people say they are not ready for Christ to come into their heart. Jesus is standing at the door knocking and you are just ignoring him and even acknowledges his presence. Your body is the house where he wants to dwell. Your temple, Jesus, is the light of the world. You turn him away and the thought of him does not enter your mind again for a long time or until something goes wrong.

Yet Satan can show up, disguise himself, knock and if no answer, knock the door down, take over your mind, soul, rule you, lie on you, and steal from you. Try to kill you every chance he gets. He bombards his way into your heart. Then you say, "I'm not ready for Christ yet". <u>Satan wants you Dead or Alive. God wants you dead in sin, and alive in Christ.</u> Therefore, it is OK for Satan, but not OK for Christ to invite himself in. Think about it. Do not wait too long. The Lord is definitely coming back.

Each day we rise, he has blessed us with new Grace and Mercy. God has equipped us with Ephesians 6:11-17, to get dressed into his suit of armor daily. God has given us Love, Peace and a Sound Mind. We call his name anytime of the day anywhere we see fit. He says in Jeremiah 33:3 if you were to call my name I will answer thee. Jesus is just a prayer away. You can call him, or better yet *Just Say Jesus*. Whisper Jesus' names several times softly. Each time sounds better than the one before. That is a beautiful name with a lovely attitude. By the way, he also says he will not withhold any of this from us. Whatever he has he is willing to share it. If you have never asked Jesus to come into your life; today is a very good day.

Do not allow Satan to be the Prince of your World.

Do allow God to Save Your Soul From the burning Hell in Jesus Name.

Do allow Jesus to be the Lord of your Life.

Ask him to become your Savior Today. (Romans 10:9)

I Pray for Lost Souls to Repent and Accept Christ as Their Savior in Jesus Name, Amen.

Jesus

CHARM

WALKING WITH CHRIST

Walking with Christ is not a stroll through the park. Holding hands with a loved one; gazing in their eyes; so high on love; intense with passion, hoping and praying never to come down, anticipating nothing and no one interfering with this precious moment. Loving and loving the thought of being loved. Moving up towards the future and leaving the past behind.

Now does that sound like an ideal stroll or walk with that special person in your life? That's the kind of relationship we should have with Christ each and every day. Seeing him in that way. Loving the idea of him holding our hand to walk through our trials and tribulations with him. Knowing and trusting that he will never leave us nor forsake us, once we have invited him in our hearts to take residence.

Heated Passion:

The heated passion along with the desire of the Lord should be so intense nothing should be able to put out the flames. When you are on fire for the lord you truly don't want that fire out. If it seems to be going out, then put in another log – by seeking him out. That will keep the passion burning. Ask to be put on fire for the Lord and his word, remember (James 4:2,3) we have not because you ask not; Vs 3-receive not because we ask for the wrong reason. As long as you have the Lord's word, which is the word of God and the Lord and Savior Jesus Christ, you will have what you need to keep the fire burning.

Being High:

Being high in the secular (natural world) can't compare to being high on the presence of the Holy Spirit. If you ever receive the baptism of the Holy Spirit, then you really would be asking not to ever come down off this high. It's something that you have to experience for yourself. No one can explain it – they can try. (**Smile**)

Remember, we are talking about a God that is bigger than anything, that has control of everything, and knows and can do all things.

Meeting:

Let's say you are in a meeting at the workplace and you are in a conference. You don't want any interference, no one calling on phone, no one talking, and definitely no distractions of any kind. When you are seeking God's face, studying his word, praying, it should be just like a conference. You're meeting with god. That rule should apply just as strict as another should. Set up an appointment daily with him, early in the morning, evening, just make sure you are setting time away to meet with him in your prayer closet. That's between you and him.

Loving:

Everybody wants to be loved and everyone should love. The greatest gift of all is love – love never fails -- love can be unconditional -- God so love the world- men love your wives- love your neighbor as you love yourself. You can not be a Christian and do not have love in your heart. Jesus is love- looking for love in all the wrong places. **Examine your heart and soul. Be honest, what do you see?**

As you know, there is love explained to us in different ways. Jesus explains it in the way we are to have it.

Love can be seen – by showing love-when his light shines in you.
Love can be spoken – when you speak the true word of god from the depth of your heart. Love can be felt in your innermost beings – soul- emotions. You can also be taught to love, when you learn Jesus'way.
You can have love the same way you can have life----eternal. Amen

Moving:

Moving up towards the future---Mmm---wonder sometimes...
Moving meaning – change position: up meaning – higher place.

When I think about moving up in the **natural** world, it comes to mind, standing in line, maybe on a waiting list or moving up in the world- material things, job, promotion, bigger expensive house, nicer clothes, etc.

Spiritual sense seems to be a little different prospect. Moving up towards the future, having a closer relationship with the spiritual father – seeing him for who he is - reverence him -giving him all the glory, honor, and praise in everything that he does in our lives. Worship him with all that is in you, in spirit and in truth.

Leaving the past behind, the old man, Adam nature, and not looking at what once was, but what God has placed before you now. Thanking him for not allowing you to forget where you came from, also looking at how he is taking you higher on his level. <u>When you really let go and let God then you have moved up to the future.</u>

That's what walking with Christ is all about.

HE'S AWESOME!!!!!!

GOD BLESS

CHARM

WHEN JESUS RETURNS WHAT WILL YOU BE DOING?

I can not say, because I don't know any more than you do, when it comes to that question. However I would like to think we (you) would be walking in the Spirit of the Lord. Galatians 5:6 speak of "wait for hope of righteousness by faith." (Meaning as believers we are empowered by the spirit through faith confidently waiting on the Lord.) I hope that you are not in a hotel room with your pants down, with someone else's spouse. Abusing drugs, needles stuck in your arm or crack cocaine pipe in your hand. Definitely not in the motion of fighting your husband or wife. Matthew 24:35-36 and 44 has a vital point that we need to really sink into our soul. This is the word of Jesus, he only speaks facts. Verse 35 reads, "Heaven and earth shall pass away, but my words shall not pass."(Vs 36) But of that **day and hour knoweth no man**, not the angels of heaven, but **my Father only**.(Vs 44)Therefore be ye also ready: for in such an hour as ye think not the Son of man cometh.

This question, "When Jesus Returns What Will You Be Doing?" It can be looked at from different points of views. If you are a true believer, worshiper, enjoy praising, trusting and have confidence in the Lord, that is delightful to God. Trusting that you are a Christian Living for God's Purpose in your life. Everyday you should be expecting the last trumpet to blow because you know your soul is at peace with God. Some of us may feel that we have what is needed to sit and wait on the trumpet. How about your family and friends? Are they ready? God is going to send Jesus in due time. Don't forget about others who are not where you are in Jesus Christ.

Well then again looking at it from another viewpoint as a person who just acknowledges God but does not reverent him in spirit and in truth. You can live your life acknowledging God, and not giving him the respect he deserves. However that is not what he is anticipating from us. All of us will have to give an account for what understanding we do have of God. The devil has you all messed up thinking that you are doing just fine. He is lying to you.

You know they still have sinners that do what they want, when they want, and how they want. I truly believe their hearts and minds are poisoned. Their tongues are spitting out nothing but lies, cursing and criticizing everyone. They are afraid to break man's law and think nothing of doing the opposite of the Law of God.

Galatians Chapter 5:19-20 speaks very clearly of the flesh that manifests in the world.

Adultery-sleeping with someone else, husband or wife.
Fornication-sex without marriage.
Uncleanness-taking care of your body.
Lewdness seducing spirits.

That's something how the first few on the list are Sexual Sins. Ephesians 5:11 calls them unfruitful Work of Darkness (Evil).

Idolatry, Sorcery, Witchcraft, Astrology.
Hatred-intense dislike.
Heresies-gossiping.
Drunkenness-over indulging in strong drink.
Darkness-absence of Holy Spirit-Opens doors for Satan.
All of these things shall not inherit the kingdom of God.
(I will ask this question again) when Jesus returns what will you be doing?

KJV-Matthew 7:13 says, "Enter ye in the strait gate: for wide is the gate, and broad is the way, that leadeth to destruction, and many there be which go in thereat".

KJV-Matthew 7:14 "Because strait is the gate and narrow is the way which leadeth unto life, and few there be that find it."

<u>**Christ is comparing the entrances and offering you a chance to make your choice to enter the way to life.**</u>

In other words, people can live for their own self-interest, whatever you decide it will cost you. Wide and broad is plenty of sins that Satan has to offer you. Such as temptation, lying, judging, overindulgence of alcohol, beer, wine, food, manipulation, controlling spirits. **You can make the choice, enter in the wide, and follow the devil's will from the list we spoke of earlier in book of Galatians 5. That will only get you to <u>one</u> unpleasant place.**

Do not sit and wonder if the gate you are going through is **Sin. Look at your life if any of us is doing any of these sins, then you do not have to wonder long. Sin is Evil. It is NOT Like GOD.** The gate that is represented here is leading to destruction in **HELL**.

Let us look at it this way, if you belong to God on the Earth, you have to deal with the devil. If you belong to the devil while on earth, he will not bother you, because he already has you. Think about it, **the decision you make with the devil can burn you for life.** I mean literally, if you do not choose God to be your God on earth, you will have eternal life with the devil. <u>He would have</u> won because he had you in bondage to his way on earth, and will have you in ***bondage in Hell is*** way.

(Matthew 7:14) The narrow gate is difficult, because you have to be obedient and you will suffer persecution (people will talk about you, lie on you, etc). It's hard if you make it hard. I'm sure there are other things in your life that you suffered and you felt it was worth it. Christ is worthier than that. With God's help, you can overcome **the wide and the broad with the straight and narrow. Sinful nature** begins to drop off, as the mind becomes strong, transformation begins to take place.

Mind is being renewed.
Soul is uplifted along with faith.
Spirit is being revitalized.

Emotions *of yours are not having a pity party; you are in control now. Since you have taken control of your emotions, your body now has the strength to endure, and you become physically fit. You begin to feel better, look better and take control of your own financial situation.*

God takes care of his people. Maybe the change is not going to happen right away, but as you keep holding on to his hand, he always comes through. Continue holding on to his promises, his word, building up your faith to trust and do not give up no matter what comes your way. He would not put more on you than you are able to tolerate. Therefore, what happens when you can't carry the load on your shoulders? He will carry the load for you, if you are willing to give it to him? Each time no matter; how many times God will definitely show up to give you what you need to run this Christian race to the finish line. Your course will be complete with him in heaven. Do you want to live for God? Then tell Satan his time is up. Make the devil angry on this day. <u>Come over to the strait and narrow gate. God is waiting for you. Give him your best.</u>

If you want to really, know what God is saying about the Ten Commandments in Exodus Chapter 20. Read the bible with God's help for understanding. They have more commandments we are to live by.<u>Do not take someone else's word. See for yourself what the Lord has to say. Seek his Face, you will meet him face to face one day.</u>

Galatians Chapter 5:19-21 gives you the different works of the flesh. Take time out and study the words that are given to you in the chapter. It will surprise you, the things we think we know. God wants us to know how important these words are to our future. He has warned us before; any one who does such things will not inherit the kingdom of God. You may enter a kingdom, but not God's. As we look further in Galatians 5:22-26 God is sharing with us the Fruit of the Spirit.

My friend God is so wonderful, as you continue into the next book of Ephesians 6:10-24. He has set you up to get dressed in a whole Armor of God. **Everyday you don't have to go outside naked and not prepared. You can be fully dressed in armor, and be prepared standing strong in the Lord.**

Jeremiah 23:23 " Am I a God at hand, saith the Lord and not a God afar off?"

Jeremiah 32:27" Behold, <u>I am the Lord, the God of all flesh:</u>is there anything too hard for me."

Glory Be To God, JESUS

CHARM

WOULD YOU DO IT?

As a mother I love my sons very dearly, I would do just about anything for my boys, they are mine. I feel the only one I have to share them with is **God.** Other than him, they're mine. You know I am just like anybody else when it comes to protecting your own, not someone else's. I feel as though I can do anything for them within reason. When I say within reason, I'm not talking about my reasoning or their reasoning, I'm talking within **God's** reasoning, his perfect will.

That's something how parents these days love their kids so much, some will cut back on groceries, lack on paying a bill, or even point blank lie just to protect that child. All of this some parents have done – going to do, and will do for this child, that they love so much. Now I hope you know this will not make the child respect them nor love them. If anything the children and the parents need discipline.

We have heard for a long time, some of us all our lives "John 3:16 for God so loved the world, he gave his only begotten son." I have a question **"Would you do it?"** Would you know your child being born, people will not tell the truth about him, and knowing deep down who he is, being tempted by the devil, betrayed, sold for 30 pieces of silver, and crucified. Crucifixion is nothing nice, in those days that was one of the lowest, dirtiest punishments you can do to anyone.

Jesus could have refused to die but he came to <u>set an example before **us**</u>. <u>He **endured** the cross – he suffered for **us** – so that **we** may have eternal life.</u> Looks like to me Jesus is <u>very concerned about **us.**</u> You know we hear people say "yeah I'm going through, or I've been there and done that, (BTDT), girl I'm still praying – it's got to be better than this. I have even heard through a conversation someone says, "life got to be better than this." Believe it or not, life can be cold and discouraging, yet life with Christ in it is a lot better than life without Christ. (Praise God)

You tell me if you would change your life to swap with Jesus. You couldn't handle what he went through. I don't believe I could either. Now there is something about someone doing well as far as materialistic things – well dressed, good attitude, decent job, and money in the bank. You may look at this person or maybe even know a person like this. What if at this time in your life you're not doing as well as they are; bill collectors calling, cars acting up along with children tripping (acting rebellious). You're assuming that this person got it going on. In reality if you only knew what this person had to go through to get to this point in their life, or how they suffered (just like Jesus) being lonely many days and nights, crying, perhaps the loss of a family member to a freak accident, or drunk driver. Could be even by one of those kids that they have spoiled with all those material things, to win their love. Don't you know the more you give them the more they want?

When a person is doing well you would change your life with them by a drop of a hat. Sometimes when you hear what's going on in their life and it's not pleasant, **you wouldn't do it.**

For example, would you give your only child to suffer – going through trials (you'll try to fix them too). Nor would you allow your child to be put to death. We have to go through to fulfill The Bible. If, maybe **God** promised you he would bring him back (resurrect). Being honest, trusting God on that would be hard for you to do.

God knew all of this was going to take place before it happened. He just did it. He did not try to compromise with God. He loved the world so much, he thought it and his response was, **just do it**. He knew what his son Jesus was going to go through. Look at what Jesus went through in 30 something years of life on this earth. Born to a virgin in a barn (not a heated hospital), he was about his father's business at a young age. He seeks God's face faithfully through prayer, Jesus also spent time with the father daily, and he was obedient to the father's will, Jesus lived for him – suffered for us. John, chapters 14-17 he prayed the longest prayer to the father, prayed for the disciples, prayed for us and he asked his Father if we can have life eternal. He asked for us knowing he was about to die.

He (God) has asked us, children of God who ever believe in him to do some little things, we say we can't or is it "we just won't because it is not our will to please a man like Jesus who died for us. Everybody thinks it's all about him or her. When you are concerned about pleasing this old wicked world, you are no better than the rest of the world. They don't care about you and no one else. Satan has a trap set, be careful you can fall in just like the world. Jesus is the only one you can trust. He promised he would never leave you nor forsake you. Now all of the things that took place and the way Jesus lived his life for that short period of time, some of us are older than he was when he died, and still hanging on by **God's** grace & mercy. Still wanting the whole party for themselves.

Each day that passed, God gave us still yet another chance to come to him. Learn to appreciate life more abundantly through Jesus Christ as your Savior.

Now that you know about what he has done for you, does that change anything in your spirit?

Do you know anybody that would die for you? How much do you love him?

Would you do it? (Give your only begotten son to save this world.)

JESUS

CHARM

THE WILL

I hope that you know there are different types of wills. Each one is very vital to our lives. We should live our lives to the fullest and stop worrying about the wrong thing. Why not think about what God has willed for your life? What is your purpose for your life? Ask God so you may be lined up in <u>his perfect will.</u> Thank God, you are alive. We should be more conscious of the Lord 's Prayer (Psalm 23) He said: Let thy will be done, not my will.

Here is one form of a will, called a living will. This will operate something like this: if you have had an accident and are unable to make intelligent decisions for yourself, the family or power of attorney will make decisions for you. While you are in your rightful state of mine, you can have papers drew up by an attorney. This way you may decide whether you want to live off a machine. If not, your family will decide what they want to do about your situation. On the condition you want to live off a machine then there is another type of will. Perhaps you may want to consider a living will. Allow me to say the ***will to live.*** Take into thought of it as the <u>second living will.</u>

Therefore, that type of will give you the desire to live. That's just another form of desire, aspiration, hope, and determination. We can have a will to live. This is one thing in particular God wants for us, the will for us to live and not die. God is the only one who can give and take a life. Accordingly, all those who have had demonic suicide attempt and have thoughts of it. God said "I give it and I taketh away". That is why you are still alive today and you are a living testimony. He has willed you to live. We should want that for ourselves anyway. He is concerned more about you than you are about yourself. He said in Proverbs I'm concerned about all of what I have created, I have counted the hairs on your head also about when you thrust your foot against the stone.

Last but not least; it is the will of inheritance, I think this is a <u>very powerful will.</u> You know the one where everybody shows up after you die to see what you left him or her of your estate. Yeah, the one that makes the covetous comes out. In other words,<u>the real you.</u> There is no need to be ashamed of them, every family has one. Greed has been waiting on someone to die. They are so bold and boastful that they are not ashamed to let you know what they are all about, they are being honest. They want everyone to know they're greedy and proud of it. In addition they're the ones who sit and <u>patiently wait or try to estimate when someone is going to die, so they can get their inheritance.</u> To speak for myself, I would rather my loved ones live forever, before I become concerned about an inheritance.

Truth of the matter, you do not have to wait on your relatives and friends to die, just to get an inheritance. <u>God has fixed it so you can inherit the Kingdom of God right now.</u> Matthew 25:34 says "Then shall the King say unto them on the right hand, Come ye blessed of my Father, inherit the kingdom prepared for you from the foundation of the world" (in the beginning). The book of Matthew 19:16-30, Jesus was speaking to a young man who had approached him asking the question" what shall he do to have eternal life?" He gave him several answers, then he gave him the final one in Matthew 19:21. "If thou be perfect,<u>go and sell </u>that thou hast, and give it to the poor, and thou shalt have treasure in heaven: and come follow me". After the young man heard this he went away sad, because he had great possessions. This young man is just like some of the people of our time; he was not willing to give up his things. It is not like Jesus wanted them, but the man failed the test that let him know where his heart truly was. When you're able to give fleshly things then you are lined up with God's desires.

It is as simple as this to inherit characteristics <u>passed on between generations</u> now you have received the inheritance to the kingdom through Jesus Christ. God gave his son power over all. Everything belongs to God, Psalm 50:10-12, I love when he says <u>the world is mine.</u> I guess because by the world belonging to him, Jesus is his son, and we are joint heirs to Christ. We are children of God by the Spirit of Adoption. We are not only the heir of God and joint heir of Christ (Romans 8:15-17). That makes our inheritance also the Kingdom of God. After accepting Christ as being born again spiritually, you should not just want to **See**the kingdom. This is my opinion, seeing the Kingdom is not enough for me. I want to enter also. It is not a good feeling on the outside looking in. John 3:3 meaning just to partake of the kingdom. **You should want to enter the kingdom (the true church), by being born of water and of spirit.** Along with that you should have a change of heart. For that reason do not get hung up on the inheritance of the world. It is only temporal; it's subject to change. The gift of God is eternal in this world and the world to come.

God has a permissive will without restriction. In addition he has his perfect will, this is a complete and excellent will. This is the will God wants to leave you is like a special two for one. You give me your life and I'll give you life eternal. Your inheritance is on earth with blessings from God. Then inheritance in heaven eternally. This is the Real Will of God.

It is not easy to live in the Will of God, but it is necessary.

THANK YOU LORD

Charm

Part III

POEMS

AMAZING GRACE

We the people have seen your Amazing Grace.
As we read and study your words we see your amazing face.

You have given us more unmerited favor.
When we accept you as our Lord and Savior.

Because of iniquity our lives have been damaged.
Without God's twins we could not manage.

He said once he entered into our heart.
He would never leave us nor depart.

Always we have heard.
He will not change his glorious words.

The day will come when we meet him face to face.
He will continue blessing us with his <u>Amazing Grace.</u>

Amen

JESUS

CHARM

DRIP!!!!

Dripping, falling of drops,

    Sometimes it seems as though it never stops.

This can be a very slow process,

    God's giving you favor can drip into success.

When the blood of Jesus dropped to the ground,

    The sky was darkening as the thunder sounded.

God dripped his love upon us, that's when it truly began.

    With his only begotten son, he blessed us again

JESUS

CHARM

EVERY MAN FOR HIMSELF

The bible says Jesus knew us when we were in our mother's womb,
He died once and was placed in a tomb.

But, Oh on the ninth hour,
Death and the Grave tried to hold him; he rose with all power.

If God told us once, He told us twice,
This is not a game where you roll the dice.

Each and everyone of us will have to give an account,
The books will open, then one book judging according to your amount.

This is for every man great and small,
Every man for himself, Jesus is coming once and for all.

In Jesus Name

CHARM

GOING AWAY

NO MATTER HOW FAR THE DISTANCE,
THE LOVE OF GOD IS ALWAYS CONSISTENT.

FROM DAY ONE AT BIRTH,
HE PROMISED TO BE WITH YOU UNTIL THE END OF
THE EARTH.

SOMETIMES WHEN THINGS SEEM LONELY AND BLUE,
REMEMBER HE SAID, "I DIDN'T BRING YOU THIS FAR TO
LEAVE YOU."

SO HOLD YOUR HEAD UP, STICK YOUR CHEST OUT,
CONTINUE BELIEVING IN YOUR HEART, JESUS IS WHO IT'S
ALL ABOUT.

BE BLESSED

CHARM

JESUS

HE IS...

HE IS
   WONDERFUL
HE IS
   GLORIOUS
HE IS
   LORD
HE IS
   SAVIOR
HE IS
   LOVE
HE IS
   GRACEFUL
HE IS
   WORTHY
HE IS
   COUNSELOR
HE IS
   GUIDANCE
HE IS
   ALPHA & OMEGA
HE IS
   AWESOME

ALL THESE WORDS THAT HE IS
WORDS CAN'T EXPLAIN...

HE IS JESUS

CHARM

ISAIAH 9:6, NEH 9:5, PHIL 2:11, ISAIAH 49:26,

HE'S ALL THAT

He's glorious - wonderful- mighty warrior,
He's all that.

He's your guidance - teacher - counselor,
He's all that.

He's a doctor - healer - deliver,
He's all that.

He's the Father – Son - and Holy Spirit,
He's all that.

He's the King of all Kings,

He's the Lord of all Lords.

He's the Savior of the World.

JESUS CHRIST

CHARM

I- ME- MY

I stretched out my hand to God in desperation, but my hand wasn't long enough.

I poured out my heart to God in prayers of desperation, but I didn't trust him enough to do the things that he is capable of doing.

I walked miles down the same road to God in desperation, but I didn't walk down the path that ordered my steps to obedience followed by guidance to his resting-place (the Heart).

I stretched out my hand; He stretched out his arms.

I poured out my heart; He poured out his blessings.

I walked the same road; He carried me the whole time.

I truly believe I had given him all that I had, but then my mind was renewed.

I realized he had given all that he had, his beloved Son, Jesus.

CHARM

IT'S ME O' LORD
STANDING IN THE NEED OF PRAYER AGAIN!

Bless me Lord Ask, ask, ask
Request, request and ask again.
God hears us, but do we hear him?

After we ignore him, then we come right back and call his name and put in another request.

How many times had we just totally ignored the lord?

Could it be countless? Being honest, all of us have fallen short in that area.

Then we ask him to answer the request again, we ask in Jesus name, speaking in utterance, anointing your bodies from the crown of your head to the soul of your feet. Well, God decides to answer your request. Yea, you thank him once, maybe even twice.

He calls upon you, and you ignore him again.

The spirit of the Lord not only rests upon you, he also blesses you. He gives you new grace and new mercy daily.

We need to give him the glory, the honor and the praise. Hearken to the Holy Spirit.
<u>Stop asking all the time.</u>
Take time to say <u>thanks</u>.
Take time to <u>receive</u> a word from the Lord.

Then you will not have to ask always, he knows your heart. He will bless you as you bless him.

Amen

JESUS

CHARM

LAST MOMENT NOTICE

Seems that at the last moment I found myself with a desperate need.
I had to look up towards heaven with a desperate plea.
All Within me somehow I knew he heard,
Even with A voice of despair and a lack of words.
I didn't know what blessings I would get,
Prayers are still being answered, you bet.
God bless you

Charm

Sometimes at the last moment we find ourselves trying to fix a desperate need. We have to look up towards heaven, and call his Holy Name. He always shows up right on time.

LOVE

Man set aside a day to show some love,
Our commandment to love comes from above.

We are to love like Jesus, three hundred sixty five,
His true love never dies; it's always alive.

Looking at your soul as a total self,
This can't be put on a shelf.

Soul ties may start as a one-time date,
Soul mates end as your destiny through fate.

We are not saying we love once a year,
To one another, we are very dear.

It's in our walk, just as well in our talk,
It's not the way we act; it's the way we react,

It's not just how we care, also in how we share.
Right from the start, Love dwelled in our hearts.

JESUS

CHARM

THANKS

When I wake up and I begin to pray,
First, I Thank God for this Blessed Day.

Entering into the gates with thanksgiving and courts with praise,
With the Lord in my life, I am truly amazed.

I also want to thank you Lord for forgiving me,
Chastisements will come, because I have sinned against thee.

Sometimes I believe my life is in such a mess,
I can still call you, because your holy name is blessed.

I thank you Lord for choosing me to be a pleasant sight,
You know my heart's desire is to shine as a light.

The times has not yet come,
To see all the things you have done.

I thank you God for winning my inner soul,
I am looking forward to walking the streets paved with gold.

In Jesus Name

CHARM

WANT TO BE

Want to be in Heaven,
>Don't want to labor to get there.

Want to be seen in church,
>Don't want to have the church in you.

Want to be forgiven for your sins,
>Don't want to forgive others of theirs.

Want to be loved,
>Don't want to give love in return.

Want to have peace and joy in your household,
>But you want to raise cain in the household of others.

Want to be looked at as an angel,
>Behind the scenes you're acting like the devil.

Want to be in Heaven,
>With that attitude, you're on your way to **Hell**.

JESUS

CHARM

YOU'RE NOT

*YOU'RE NOT FIT TO LIVE,
AND YOU'RE SURELY NOT FIT TO DIE.*

*YOU'RE NOT SERVING THE LIVING GOD - JESUS, THEN
YOU'RE NOT SERVING GOD.*

*YOU'RE NOT TELLING THE TRUTH, THEN YOU'RE NOT
LIVING THE TRUTH YOU MUST BE LIVING A LIE.*

*YOU'RE NOT WALKING IN THE GODLY SPIRIT,
YOU MUST BE WALKING HOLDING ON TO SATAN'S SPIRIT.*

*YOU'RE NOT LOVING OR SHOWING LOVE,
YOU MUST BE SHOWING BITTERNESS, ENVY, JEALOUSY
AND STRIFE.*

*YOU'RE NOT WALKING IN LIGHT, YOU MUST BE WALKING
IN DARKNESS.
YOU'RE NOT GIVING; YOU MUST BE ON THE BEGGING &
RECEIVING END, WITH YOUR HAND OUT. (JESUS HAND IS
OUT TOO, TO WELCOME YOU IN THE KINGDOM.)*

*YOU'RE NOT READING - WATCHING AND PRAYING,
YOU MUST BE READING JUNK, WATCHING TV & PRAYING TO
THE WRONG GOD.*

*YOU'RE NOT ALIVE, UNTIL CHRIST IS ALIVE IN YOU.
YOU'RE NOT DOING WITHOUT HIM, BECAUSE WITHOUT
HIM YOU CAN'T DO NOTHING-BUT WITH HIM YOU CAN DO
ALL THINGS.*

I'M GOING TO LEAVE YOU WITH A THOUGHT:

IF YOU MET ME & FORGOT ME, YOU HAVE LOST NOTHING, BUT IF YOU MET JESUS & FORGOT HIM, YOU HAVE LOST EVERYTHING.

IF YOU'RE NOT FIT TO LIVE RIGHT, LOVE RIGHT AND TREAT PEOPLE RIGHT.

YOU'RE NOT FIT FOR HEAVEN,

BUT SATAN WILL BE HONORED TO FIT YOU INTO HELL. (WITH A SMILE).

JESUS

CHARM

Just A Little Something Extra

This is a poem I wrote for you:

Roses are red, Violets are blue, you are so sweet, and I love you. No-No-that's not going to go through your heart, I will try this again. Here I go.

SEASONS OF LOVE

This is the beginning of our hearts,
We realize it is hard for us to depart.

When it rain, you are my sunshine,
That is our hearts intertwined.

Summer months have come and gone,
The love we share is standing strong.

When the leaves began to drop,
Our inner sensations begin to pop.

Snow is your voice; as my soul melts,
Only you and I know what is being felt.

Listen, music playing as hearts flutter,
Not one word has to be uttered.

Seasons are subject to change,
True love knows this love is not strange.

It does not matter if it's summer or fall,
God has given us the faith to handle it all.

Now as the arrows of Love takes its aim,
The Season of Love remains the same.

CHARM

OUR FIRST

HOPE & PRAY IT'S NOT OUR LAST,
OUR LIFE TOGETHER SHALL BE A BLAST.

GOD HAS GIVEN US ANOTHER CHANCE,
THAT SHOULD MAKE US WANT TO SHOUT & DANCE.

EVERY TIME THE LIAR IS TRYING TO SIFT,
GOD MEETS US & GIVES US A LIFT.

WE BOTH APPRECIATE GOD'S MERCY & GRACE,
THAT'S WHAT HELP KEEPS US IN OUR PLACE.

AS WE BEGIN TO LOVE AND SHARE,
GOD REMINDS US HOW MUCH HE CARES.

AS TIME PAST, I HAVE HAD WORST,
AS GOD CONTINUE TO BLESS, I THANK HIM THAT
WE'RE ABLE TO
SHARE OUR FIRST.

AMEN

GOD BLESS ALWAYS

CHARM

THE DAY

This is the day that the Lord hath made,

We will rejoice and be glad in it.

This day is important to some, Not so important to others.

This is the day the Lord hath made.

You can choose to do whatever is pleasing,

Remember, prayer without ceasing.

This is the day that the Lord hath made.

Now I can go out and buy you an expensive gift at a cheap price,

But I could never compare to God,

whom choose this day to give you,

The precious gift of life.

Happy Birthday

God Bless You

CHARM

Just A Thought

CHILDREN LEARN WHAT THEY LIVE

If a child lives with criticism
he learns to condemn.

If a child lives with hostility
he learns to fight.

If a child lives with ridicule
He learns to be shy.

If a child lives with shame
he learns to feel guilty.

If a child lives with tolerance
He learns to be patient.

If a child lives with encouragement
He learns confidence.

If a child lives with praise
he learns to appreciate.

If a child lives with fairness
he leans justice.

If a child lives with security
he learns to have faith.

If a child lives with approval
he learns to like himself.

If a child lives with acceptance & friendship
He learns to find love in the world.

Anonymous

CHARM

THE LORD'S PRAYER

OUR FATHER:
    Begin praying by taking time to love your heavenly Father.
WHICH ART IN HEAVEN:
    Reflect on His character.
HALLOWED BE THY NAME:
    Praise Him for who He is.
THY KINGDOM COME:
    Ask GOD for an awakening of His plan for your life.
THY WILL BE DONE IN EARTH, AS IT IS IN HEAVEN:
    Pray for loved ones, neighbors and leaders around the country.
GIVE US THIS DAY OUR DAILY BREAD:
    Lift up your personal needs to GOD.
AND FORGIVE US OUR DEBT AS WE FORGIVE OUR DEBTORS:
    Confess your sins to GOD and forgive others who have wronged you.
AND LEAD US NOT INTO TEMPTATION:
    Examine your plans and pray that your life is pleasing to the LORD.
BUT DELIVER US FROM EVIL:
    Confront the strongholds in your life and pray for deliverance.
FOR THINE IS THE KINGDOM, AND POWER, AND THE GLORY FOREVER:
    Worship GOD and thank Him for His everlasting goodness.

AMEN.

ANONYMOUS

References

Holy Bible containing Old and New Testament King James Version Copyright 19945 Broadman and Holman Publishers, Nashville, TN 37234

New Revised Standard Version Bible contains Old and New Testaments Copyright 1989 Zondervan Publishing House. Grand Rapids, Mi 49530

About the Author

I was born and raised in New Orleans, La. I have resided in Greensboro, NC since 1986. I was a single parent, a blessed mother of two sons. I have been an active member of East White Oak Missionary Baptist Church. I have attended two years of Extension from Shaw Divinity College.

www.ingramcontent.com/pod-product-compliance
Lightning Source LLC
LaVergne TN
LVHW091555060526
838200LV00036B/847